AF531303

NAXALISM
ISSUES AND CONCERNS

NAXALISM
ISSUES AND CONCERNS

Edited by

Dr. Dasarathi Bhuyan
Deptt. of Political Science
Bellaguntha Science College
Distreict- Ganjam
Brahmapur University (Orissa)

&

Dr. Amit Kumar Singh
R.S.M.(P.G.) College
Dhampur, Bijnor
(U.P.)

DISCOVERY PUBLISHING HOUSE PVT. LTD.
NEW DELHI-110 002

First Published-2010
Reprinted: 2013
ISBN 978-81-8356-597-4

Published by:
DISCOVERY PUBLISHING HOUSE PVT. LTD.
4831/24, Ansari Road, Prahlad Street
Darya Ganj, New Delhi-110002 (India)
Phone: +91-11-23279245, 43764432 • Fax: +91-11-23253475
E-mail: parul.wasan@gmail.com
info@discoverypublishinggroup.com
web: www.discoverypublishinggroup.com

Printed at:
Dynamic Printers, Delhi

PREFACE

Currently Naxalism has been branded as India's biggest internal security problem. Naxalism can be acknowledged as a particular set of terrorism at the internal level of the country. In this crucial moment it is not necessary to deliberate over the issue of weather Naxalism is a socio-economic problem or a law and order problem, reasonably it is high time to outline the root causes. Naxalism has been described in the country as the biggest internal security challenges. Therefore, it is high time to draft a national policy for its completely suppression from the Indian soil. In the beginning Naxal movement was launched to safeguard interests of innocent and poor people but later on it has diverted from its original aim. Indeed, today Naxalism is another name of terrorism for hampering peace and destroying law and order of the country. It is in the most neglected areas of the country that Left-wings extremism thrives today. These are also the main recruiting grounds for Naxalite outfits. Almost half of the Indian territories have been affected by Naxalism converting them into "Liberation Zones" and taking upon themselves the functions of the state administration and police. Without effective law and order, economic development would be impossible.

The Naxal insurgency in India is an area of increased concern in terms of intensity of violence, militarization, linkages with secessionist groups, and efforts to generate mass support. The Naxalites operate in a vacuum created due to an absence of administrative and political institutions; thereby the exploited segments of the population seek an alternative system of governance through the butt of gun. The Naxal movement in India can presently be classified into three phases – *organization phase, guerrilla warfare phase and mobile warfare phase*. In the *Organization stage*, Maoist cadres concentrate on building up agitations on people's issues and violence is extremely selective (strategic defensive). In the *guerrilla phase*, the revolutionaries see themselves to be on an equal footing with the state and fight for area domination. This is the stage where violence reaches a climax, as the rebels' attacks on security forces (strategic stalemate). *The mobile warfare phase* is one where the rebels control the area and the security forces are forced to be on permanent guard (strategic offensive). It is difficult to demarcate the areas state-wise, as there is bound to be a large overlap among the three phases. However, the Left Wing Extremist (LWE) movement in the Bastar forest areas of Chhattisgarsh is undoubtedly in the mobile warfare stage, where revolutionaries and people's militia clearly have an upper hand over the security forces.

After the independence various programmes were introduced for the development rural areas. But due to feudal nature of the bureaucrats, governmental authority, complex rules and regulations, corruption, administrative dullness and the lack of general awareness, the real benefit of development process limited within few selfish groups and people. The land reforms could not implement effectively. The very fact that land reforms as a State subject has disappeared from Indian policy-making in the age of economic liberalization. The announced targets during Five-year Plans achieved to the very limited extent. Moreover, the policies of LPG (Liberalization, Privatization and Globalization) initiated in 1991 acknowledged the social-economic inequality as the binding part of development process. The state's anti-poverty programmes such as the Natinal Democratic Alliance (NDA)

Food-for-Work or the United Prograsive Alliance (UPA) established Employment Guarantee Programme hardly met the basic demand for land rights in rural India. The rise of backward castes to power in Bihar, Uttar Pradesh and elsewhere, even though it may have democratized certain aspects of the polity, has had the paradoxical effect of freezing land relations. All these have kept the Naxal agenda alive.

India's North-East is a region is packed in between Bhutan, China, Myanmar (Burma) and Bangladesh. More then 220 ethnic groups live there, all of them with an age-old history, their own culture, custom, religion and language. After India attained Independence in 1947 the multi-faced North-East was divided and accordingly seven States - Assam, Meghalaya, Tripura, Mizoram, Arunachal Pradesh, Nagaland, and Manipur were formed. Many christened them as "seven sisters". Political movements for autonomy or separate nationhood of certain ethnic groups have been quite frequent in the "seven sisters". No other movement in independent India has proved so stubborn. Despite their division into seven units, there is no complete peace. This is also a major internal security challenge.

Therefore, the internal security challenges like - Naxalism, Maosit movement, ethnicity and regionalism in North-East India, has to be fought at various fronts such as security, ideological, social and economic. The administrations of respective states, central government and the security agencies have to co-ordinate the operations. Local population has to be taken into confidence and self-help groups should be formed.

The Central Government has prepared a comprehensive 14-point plan to deal with the problem. There have been special emphasis on the socio-economic development of the affected areas, and the state governments have been asked to ensure speedy implementation of land reforms. The national tribal policy seeks to protect the rights of tribals. But these measures are not adequate to tackle the problem of Naxalism.

Naxalism is one of the major challenges to our nation building. There is no doubt that through enlightened policies and commitment these challenges would be over come. It is, however, essential to ensure that this is achieved with minimum dissonance, human tragedies and loss of lives, so that the transformation of those at the margins of our economic success story is as painless as possible.

A comprehensive discussion has been made in this volume by eminent research scholars to create a common consensus to find the roots of Naxalism and eliminate its evil menace. This volume contains highly research-oriented articles/papers contributed by eminent social scientists, research scholars, professors and academicians. We are extremely thankful to all the contributors for their kind collaboration, cooperation, deep faith and trust on the editors.

Our sincere thanks are also due to Sri Tilak Wasan, Director of M/s Discovery Publishing House Pvt. Ltd, New Delhi, who extended his incredible help for publishing this volume. We are sure that this volume will fully ensure the academic needs of the researchers, scholars, readers, social activists, political decision-makers, bureaucrats for solving the Naxal problem in India.

Dasarathi Bhuyan
Amit Kumar Singh

CONTENTS

LIST OF CONTRIBUTORS

Dr. Alka R. Gupta holds a doctorate in Political Science from Banaras Hindu University on India and Pakistan: Security Concerns. She is a Sr. Lecturer and among the youngest Head of the PG department of Political Science at Udai Pratap Autonomous College, Varanasi. This College is known as the pioneer of the educational institutions in eastern Uttar Pradesh as well as the first autonomous college of the State. She has written several articles on burning issues in several reputed journals and magazines. Besides she is engaged in drafting a book based on India's regional policy with special reference to Pakistan. She has conducted a survey on the role and interest of the youth in Indian politics. She has participated in various national and international seminars, conferences and workshops and presented papers on the forum. Often she conducts extra-curricular programmes for the youth. Author is associated with Malviya Centre for Peace Research which works on global peace and its varied dimensions. Also with Malviya Centre for Ethics and Values which focuses on Mahamana's values in public life. She is a dedicated persona in the field of moral re-armament and revival of moral ethics. She is associated with Nehru Youth Hostel as a coordinator in voluntary capacities. In addition she is among the major facilitator of Gandhi

Vidya Sansthan, Rajghat which propogates Mahatma Gandhi's values and ideas worldwide. She is associated with College for Teacher's Education - a government training centre for TGT and PGT teachers as a resourse person. She is a member of Companion Society - an international NGO - especially related with women empowerment and communal harmony. Above all author is a devoted social scientist and is known for her dynamism.

Dr. Amit Kumar Singh, posted at R.S.M.(P.G.) College, Dhampur, Bijnor, U.P. has been teaching since eight years. He obtained his Masters Degree and Ph.D. from Banaras Hindu University. His area of specialization includes, International Relation, Conflict Resolution, Globalization, Human Security and Human Development. He has participated in more than 25 international and national conferences and seminars and presented paper in them. He has published several articles in books, journals, magazines and newspapers. He has written three books: *Indo-Pak Relations*, *New Perspective, Globalization and Indian, Globalization: Peace and Media*. He is a member of different learned bodies such as South Asia Foundation, IDSA, New Delhi. Indian Association of Political Science. Presently, he is also Research Associate in Indian Institute of Advance Studies, Shimla.

Dr. Ashutosh Pandey, is presently working in P.G. Department of Political Science, Amar Singh (P.G) College, Lakhaoti, Bulandshahr (CCS University, Meerut). He got his D.Phil in Political Science, from University of Allahabad. He has published several research articles in different journals and books. His area of specialization includes Indian Government and Politics, Grassroots Politics, Women Empowerment, Ecology and Human Rights, and Public Administration. He has been a member of several learned associations such as IPSA, IIPA, ISSA, ISGS, and UPPSA. He has participated in several national/international seminars and conferences and presented papers in them. Currently he is pursuing a UGC-sponsored research project on "Relevance of Mahatma Gandhi in Global Era: A Case Study".

Dr. Bishnu Narayana Sethi is a scholar in social sciences. He received his Ph.D. degree from Brahmapur University. The author is a young economist, a keen researcher, presented number of articles to national and international magazines and seminars. Author of *Labour Out Migration in Orissa*, member of board of studies M/s Sultan Chand and Sons. He is presently working as a Lecturer in Economics, Laxmi Narayan Degree College, Kodala, Distt. Ganjam, Orissa.

Dr. Dasarathi Bhuyan, a familiar Odiya writer, has numerous publications to his credit. He has published 5 volumes of short stories in Odiya - *Pragatir Chaka Tale* (Beneath the wheel of progress), *Maachha Akhir Luha* (Eye tears of a fish), *Mulyahin Swadhinata* (Worthless freedom), Aloda Manish (Unwanted man) and *Dukha* (Sorrow). He has also published one volume of poems - *Milan Muhurta* (the meeting moment), one volume of columns - *Nirvachita Sthambha* (selected columns) and one volume of Novel - *Janma Janmantara* (Birth and Rebirth). He has also been publishing a literary magazine *Bhinnaswar*. In addition to these he has written a number of books in English: *Casteism in Indian Politics*, Anmol Publications, New Delhi, *Women Empowerment*, Discovering Publishing House, New Delhi, *J.B. Patnaik: A Political Biography,* Indian Publishers Distributors, Delhi, *Naveen Patnaik: the Best Chief Minister,* Indian Publishers Distributors, Delhi, *Role of Regional Political Parties in India,* M/s Mittal Publications, New Delhi, *Women in Politics*, M/s Discovery Publishing House Pvt. Ltd., New Delhi, *International Terrorism*, M/s Mohit Publications, New Delhi, *International Politics*, Nalanda, Cuttack, *Kalahandi Ke Log* (Translated), Sanjaya Book Centre, Varanasi. He has received a number of awards for his literary achievements. Currently he is working as the Head, department of political science, Bellaguntha Science College, District Ganjam, Orissa under Brahmapur University.

Dr. Deepak Kumar Pandey, M.A. Ph.D in Political Science from B.H.U. Varanasi (Gold Medal). He worked on Human Security, Conflict Resolution, regional groupings in International Relations and on State politics. He participated and presented papers in more than 30 national and international seminars and conferences. Various articles have been published in English and Hindi dailies and journals (of Political Science). Presently, he is working as lecturer in Political Science at Government Degree College, Barkot, Uttarkashi, Uttarakhand.

Dr. Jayant Kumar Parida is a scholar of outstanding in Political Science. He has participated and presented a number of research papers in different national seminars. Various articles have been published in English and Oriya dailies and journals. He has also published course-based Political Science Books. Presently, he is working as lecturer in Political Science at Government College, Bhadrak, Orissa.

Manas Behera is a faculty member of Deptt. of Political Science, Government Women's College, Sundargarh, Orissa. She has participated in various national and international seminars, conferences and workshops and presented papers on the forum.

Dr. Priyankar Upadhyaya currently Professor and Director at the Malaviya Centre for Peace Research at Banaras Hindu University holds a Ph.D. and M.Phil. Degree from Jawaharlal Nehru University; Advance International Diploma(s) in Conflict Resolution from the Uppsala University, Sweden (in 1989 & again in 2005) and has done post-doctoral research at London and Ulster University and the Woodrow Wilson Centre for International Scholars, Washington DC. Has been a Faculty of Banaras Hindu University for over 28 years as a Lecturer, Reader and Professor teaching international relations and conflict resolution at Master's level and guiding research (has supervised about 20 Ph.D.s). Since March 1997, Dr Upadhyaya has been working full time Professor and Director of Malaviya Centre for Peace Research (MCPR) - an inter-disciplinary centre within the Faculty of Social Sciences.

Mr. Rajib Lochan Panigrahy is a research writer of Social Science, Management topics. He has 14 books and 20 articles in social sciences, management and business administration, information technology, published to his credit. He is working as Faculty (MBA) at Ambedkar College of Management and Technology (ACMT), Berhampur, Ganjam, Orissa.

Dr. Uddipan Mukherjee, is a Ph.D. in Physics from the Tata Institute of Fundamental Research, Mumbai. He has qualified the Indian Civil Services (ICS) examinations in 2007 with an All India Rank of 210 with History and Political Science as the subjects. Presently, he is a Lecturer in Physics at the B P Poddar Institute of Management and Technology, Kolkata.

Dr. Usha Padhy, is a scholar of outstanding in Political Science. She has participated and presented a number of research papers in different national seminars. She is presently working as a senior lecturer in Political Science at Sabitri Women's College, Bhanjanagar, District Ganjam, Orissa.

Dr. Saroja B., Lecturer and Head. Deptt. of Post Graduation Studies in Political Science, Government First Grade College, Bellary, Karnataka. She has completed her MA in Political Science from Gulbarga University, Gulbarga, Karnataka, with first Rank along with four gold medals. Completed her Ph.D. from the same university. She has written and edited several books. Her articles were published both in national as well as international journal. She has also presented many papers at the conferences and attended numerous seminars. She has been continuously engaged in research and writing.

level and guiding research. He has supervised about 20 Ph.D.s. Since March 1997, Dr. Upadhyaya has been working full-time Professor and Director of Malaviya Centre for Peace Research (MCPR) – an inter-disciplinary centre within the Faculty of Social Sciences.

Mr. Rajib Lochan Panigrahi is a research writer of Social Science, Management topics. He has 14 books and 30 articles in social sciences, management and business administration, information technology published to his credit. He is working as Faculty at Ambedkar College of Management and Technology (ACMT), Berhampur, Ganjam, Orissa.

Mr. Lakshman Mukherjee has a Ph.D. in Physics from the Tata Institute of Fundamental Research, Mumbai. He has qualified the Indian Civil Services (I.A.S. examinations) in 2007 with an All India Rank of 70 with History and Political Science as the subjects. Presently, he is a Lecturer in Physics at the B.P. Poddar Institute of Management and Technology, Kolkata.

Dr. Usha Padhy is a scholar of outstanding in Political Science. She has participated and presented a number of research papers in different national seminars. She is presently working as a senior lecturer in Political Science at Jawaharlal Nehru College, Bhanjanagar, District Ganjam, Orissa.

Dr. Saroja B. is Reader and Head, Dept. of Post Graduation Studies in Political Science, Government First Grade College, Bellary, Karnataka. She has completed her MA in Political Science from Gulbarga University, Gulbarga, Karnataka, with first Rank along with four gold medals. Completed her Ph.D. from the same university. She has well-prepared edited several books. Her many articles were published both in national as well as international journal. She has also presented many papers at the conferences and attended numerous seminars. She has been continuously engaged in research and writing.

1

NAXALISM AND INTERNAL SECURITY ANXIETIES

Priyankar Upadhyaya

The continuing surge in Naxal violence has been lately securitized at the highest level across the political spectrum. While L.K. Advani dubbed Naxalism "the Worst enemy of the Indian Dream", Prime Minister Manomahan Singh branded Naxalism as the 'single biggest threat to India's internal security' and the 'Indian way of life'. Following the official cue, the print and visual media have joined the fray to highten the Naxal scare in popular imagination. The terms like 'Red Corridor' or 'Compact Revolutionary Zone' have become a common parlance denoting the Maoist sway over a large stretch of Indian Territory including many "Dandakaranya Liberated Zones".[1]

How critical is the Naxal threat? Why should the Indian leadership, having dealt with several insurgencies and secessionist challenges, accord such priority to a rebellion based on an outmoded ideology? Is it the spurt of military style actions by the CPI (Maoist) as also the growing salience of Maoists in neighbouring Nepal that created the panic? Or is this the manifestation of a new official strategy to build public consensus in favour of 'tough and stern action' against the Maoists? Or else such secularization is imperative to tackle a complex problem warranting urgent and extra-ordinary measures on both security as well as developmental issues.

Author has urged in this paper that such securitization can work both ways. The raised security anxieties may create a backdrop to undertake much needed emergency measures at all levels; conversely it may obfuscate the generic issues, diminishing the prospects of long-term problem solving. Such exploitation draws some ideas from the theoretical construct of securitization (and de-securitization) proposed by Barry Buzan, Ole Waever and others of the Copenhagen School.[2] The framework holds that by uttering; security at state representative moves a particular development into specific area, and thereby claims a special right to use whatever means are necessary to block it. Accordingly the 'scrutinizing speech acts' (such as the single biggest internal security threat to Indian dreams/Indian way of life/and Red Corridor) have raised the level of Naxal issues to an 'existentialist threat' justifying 'emergency' beyond the normal spectrum of political process. However, the politicians tend to evoke 'securitizing speech acts' to hoist the spectre of an existential threat for electoral gains or as a diversionary method or to curtail the democratic rights on the name of national security."[3] Against such scenarios, the 'desecuritization process' could be an effective option to transfer the securitized issue back from an emergency mode or "threat-defence sequence' to a normal political process.

ANATOMY OF NAXAL VIOLENCE

The sustained influence of Maoism in India notwithstanding its decline in the land of its origin is rather symptomatic of the state of democracy and development in this country. Obviously, the appeal of Naxalism is not as much due to its ideological appeal but due to ground realities in different regions. The Naxalites might be following the Maoist trajectories of guerilla warfare but their tracks include such acts of civil violence and terror, which do not fit into any ideological pattern. In any case, now the Indian Naxalities neither claim to follow the Chinese model nor keep any connection with the Communist Party of China whom they denounce as revisionist after the reforms policies in 1978. Is the ideology being used as a subterfuge in this case? What explains the "so-called" mobilization capacity of Maoists? Is it the lure of alternate governance or are such reported arrangements based on the barrel of gun?

The Naxalite movement, starting with a peasant uprising at Naxalbari in Darjeeling District of West Bengal four decades ago has undergone varied political and organizational transferences and in the process has acquired its own Indian recipe of revolution.[4] Despite being almost wiped out in the seventies, the Naxal impulse has not succumbed to either the democratic possibilities or the brute power of Indian state. The inspirational influence of Naxalism continues to entice new disciples especially in the tribal belt seeking social justice through violence. It now embraces a range of groups, having different routes to liberate India from the clutches of feudalism and imperialism through a 'people's democratic revolution'.[5] According o estimates, between 10,00 and 20,000 battle-tested Maoists are in possession of firearms and the means to produce and procure them.[6] "Of the various armed factions, the two biggest - People's War Group (PWG) and the Maoist Communist Centre (MCC), have merged and formed the CPI (Maoist) Party in September 2004.

There is a general view that as exploitation, artificially depressed wages, iniquitous socio-political opportunities, diminishing job prospects, languishing agriculture, geographical isolation and lack of land reforms incite the growth of Naxalite movement.[7] On the other hand, the democratic deficit as reflected in unresponsive governance and local administration, crimilisation of politics, unreformed police force and a clogged judicial system incapable of dealing with the increased land disputes provide a ready context to undermine the credentials of the Indian state. With such backdrop, it is indeed difficult to convince the suffering masses that real power flows from the ballot box and not from the bullets. A senior bureaucrat from Bihar attributed the growth of Naxalism in the following metaphors: failure of law and order, ambiguity of social policy, fallings of democratic processes, failure of party system, and deficits of governance.[8]

The globalization of the Indian economy has further led to an increasing development deficit in terms of basic human needs; while the question of land redistribution has taken a back seat. The already depleting forest resources in the country are being commercialized and industrialized; mining and the construction of big dams have displaced tribals without proper resettlement policies. No wonder the spread of Naxal impulses has taken place in tribal belts conspicuous for the lowest development indicators. It is the mix of extreme poverty, different or even exploitative state machinery and oppressive feudal/business elites that has been at the core of the Maoist insurgency. The skewed development policy of the government has hardly brought any, meaningful gains for the indigenous people. Conversely, the state and its various agents have exploited them, violated their rights at whim and robbed them not just of resources but also their very human dignity.[9]

The impoverished and oppressed masses distraught by a massive transfer of forest and agricultural land for developing industry, mining, and infrastructure facilities thus readily provide fertile ground for the growth of rebellion.[10] Naxalism despite an unrealistic ideology, an outdated political program and an indiscrete application of violence, still arrests the imagination of disaffected indigenous population. Having lost faith in governmental machinery, these distraught people with shrinking access to forest resources readily look up to the Maoists to protect them against corrupt officials, exploitative traders and money lenders. Often it does not matter if the people have joined the Naxal movement willingly or not. Mostly they are inveigled in the group without understanding its full ramification and once branded as Naxalite, there is no easy exit route.[11] The local police instead of offering any succour only add to their harassment. In course, they might feel trapped between the Naxalites and State, wherein it is neither safe to support the Maoists nor turn them away.

But, instead of facilitating the development in the poorest areas, the Naxal violence only undermines it. While the enemy image of the State prohibits the functioning of basic facilities such as schools, electricity, water, health centres; the road construction and communication channels are opposed by the Naxals for tactical reasons. The conflict-evoked binaries further diminish the space for democratic assertions seeking basic human needs, as those daring to question the government on any ground are liable to be branded as a Naxalite. Indeed, "it is ironic that a movement which promises, 'Liberation' can actually end up making people less free in some ways."[12]

Unlike terrorist streak, Naxalites have not shown much inclination to directly threaten urban India. But there is no doubt that the rampant armed guerrilla attacks in rural areas are becoming deadly and with greater military trappings. Inspired by the military success of their counterparts in Nepal, there is an upsurge in the episodes of land mining and ambushes of police and Para-military vehicles as also on police stations and jails. These attacks not only target the police or government officials but also the civilians from within and outside their ranks. Indeed the spree of mindless violence has undermined much of their revolutionary credentials. Naxalites like many other rebel groups permit loot and extortion ostensibly to meet their organizational needs but often it becomes the main activity in collusion with corrupt politicians, policemen. They are also prone to host a range of anti-national activities such a illicit, narcotic trade and smuggling of counterfeit currency as well as cross-border linkages for arms procurement and training.

INTERNATIONAL DIMENSIONS

Notwithstanding the occasional insinuations of collusion with Pakistan, the Naxalites are generally bereft of any significant foreign involvement. Gone are though days when china's people's daily at the height of Cultural Revolution had called the Naxal uprising as 'a peal of spring thunder'. Today's china does not identify itself with the so-called followers of their erstwhile leader. Chinese ambassador to India, Sun Yuxi in a recent statement expressed has country's willingness to help India to crush its nagging Maoist insurgency that it once actively supported. 'if there is any help from us to Indian to get rid of them' we will try to do our best, if they call themselves Maoists, we can't stop that way but definitely it (the Maoist movement in Indian) dose not have any connection with the government of china".[13]

The United States government has reportedly shown interest in the conflict against the Naxal. A senior official of the Chhattisgrah government B.K.S. Ray held a meeting on 25 may 2006 with two officials of the US consulate in Mumbai, and reportedly welcomed an offer of held to de-mine thousands of landmines planted by rebels and training to state police personnel and humanitarian aid to about 50,000 tribal people displaced since June 2005.[14]

However, the possible nexus between the Naxalites and Nepalese Maoists has lately caused rightful security concerns. Bihar alone has eight districts with 54 police stations situated along the 753 kilometre-long open border with Nepal. However, there is not much that is happening between the two groups across borders offered its tacit support to the Maoist line on multi-party democracy, Nepal's top Maoist leader, Prachanda, in an interview to the Hindu agreed that the logic of his party's line on multi-party democracy should also apply to the Maoist movement in India.[15]

DEMOCRATIC PROMISE

With Naxalism casting a long shadow, the government has finally woken up to the imperative of a coordinated and multi-faceted approach to address the problem. The annual report 2005-06 of the union Ministry of Home Affairs accepts that '(i)t is not merely a law and order problem but has deep socio-econmic development of Naxal areas is being pursued to effectively tackle this menace.[16]

Though infested with corruption and misgovernance, the democratic structure in India have not exhausted all possibilities to wean away the poor tribals from the murky path of violence.

It would be unfair to say that the democratic governance has been totally unresponsive to the imperatives of social and economic transformation in the tribal belts. The carving out of smaller States of Chhattisgarh, Jharkhand and Uttarakhand, extension of Panchayat Raj programme to tribal areas and *Nationalist Rural Employment Guarantee Scheme* (NREGA) are some of the welcome steps to empower the indigenous population. However, it is important not to evade the issue of land reforms in rural and tribal India, which has been the trend in the post-liberalization era. It is hard to ignore the fact that the sustained campaign for land reform in West Bengal has been a critical factor in preempting the resurgence of Naxal rebellion in the place of its birth.

The real challenge however is to implement the government initiatives without allowing corrupt officials, local contractors and mafia to swipe off the development aid. The Panchayat Raj structures also need to be cleansed from unscrupulous elements and urgent steps undertaken to restore the rights of indigenous people over hand and forest. However all this requires greater coordination between the different state and central agencies.

MILITARY PREPAREDNESS

In addition to the democratic measures, the government is also gearing up to meet the challenge militarily. While the help of Army is being sought to train the police force,[17] "a 14,000 personnel strong special *anti-Maoist combat force* is being planned by next year to tackle the ultra-Leftist insurgents in 13 States. The force would comprise 9,000 personnel of central Para-military and State Police Forces and 5,000 ex-servicemen trained in fighting terrorism and dealing with improvised explosive devices (IED) and mines. The special force is undergoing training in specialized Army Camps in Bihar, Jharakhand, Chhattisgarh, Orissa, and Uttar Pradesh.[18] There are reports that Indian Air Force (IAF) has been tipped to fly reconnaissance missions over Naxal strongholds in Central India, where the writ of Government has seemingly been eroded. The IAF will fly Heron unmanned aerial vehicles to assist police and Para-military forces in tracking movements of rebels. There are suggestions to educate legislators in national security issues and also to develop an effective system of security management, which was recognized by the Administrative Reforms Commission over three decades ago.[19]

COUNTERING VIOLENCE

Realizing the inadequacy of conventional ways to meet the challenge of guerilla warfare, new ideas such as intelligence-based counterstrategy with superior weapons and operational initiatives of coercive counterinsurgency are being emulated from similar experiences elsewhere. It is in this context that the Chhattisgarh government has sought the services of K.P.S. Gil, former Police Chief of Punjab and Founder Director of Institute of Conflict Management. Several states have raised Special Forces and also explored the option of promoting the counter, violence of the locals. The creation of Girijan Greyhound by Andhra government, the infamous 'Ranavir Sena' of Upper Castes in Bihar and 'Salva Judam' are some of the counter Naxal initiatives launched in recent times.

The case of Salva Judum could be instructive to disentangle the dilemma and faultiness of the approach of counter violence. Interestingly the term 'Salva Judum' means the "Peace Campaign" in Halbi and "Collective Haunting" in the Santhali language. No wonder while the Chhattisgarh Government finds it a "non-violent movement against exploitation" the Naxal ridicule it as the group hunting of innocent tribals supporting the people's movement. Although ordinary tribals in reaction to the Naxal atrocities launched the Salva Judum, the government and other political parties soon patronized it.[20] Its campaign and retaliation by the Maoists has however exposed tribals to greater violence and displaced them in their own land.[21] The worse is that Salva Judum did not escape the accusation of institution, extortion, rape and murder.[22]

The Salva Judam campaign has raised acrimonious debates about the long-term implication of such official sponsorship of armed militants. For it is difficult on the part of the government to justify the outsourcing of its basic law and order maintance responsibility back to citizens.

WALKING ON TWO LEGS

The recent securitization evoked by the top leadership could be a good strategy not only to improve the security management measures but also to raise the issues of land reforms and poverty alleviation beyond usual platitudes to an emergency mode facilitating extraordinary remedial measures. Accordingly Manmohan Singh has recently talked about the dual strategy of "walking on two legs" - rapid development and pro-active policing to meet the growing 'sense of alienation and deprivation' among large sections of poor tribals.

But there are apprehensions that the raised security anxieties instead of according due attention to the generic causes of the conflict would only be used to justify tough police action. Even in official projections "the sustained and effective' police action finds pride of place, while 'accelerated socio-economic development' is reduced to a small section that emphasizes advice to the State governments for the Purpose.[23] The Prime Minister's call to ". . . protect policemen from undue harassment for actions taken against Naxalites", therefore needs to be supplemented with sincere efforts to preempt the violations of democratic rights and harassment of ordinary citizens.

But this is easier said then done. The hitherto dominant state-centric paradigm of security does not easily accord precedence to the protection of social dignity of common people. Echoing this imperative, a leading public figure in India has put it accurately. '(F)ronties of a State are important but so are frontiers of human dignity'.[24] Thus it is important is to include the impulse of human security issues within the existing security framework.

REFERENCES

1. According to Media Speculations, by 2010, 30 per cent of Indian Territory from the Indo-Nepal Border All the Way Down to the Southern Sate of Andhra Pradesh could Become Part of the "Red-Corridor". Different Naxal Groups now Control 19 per cent of India's Forests over an Area Two and Half Times the Size of Bangladesh. http://www.Idia-defence.com.reprts/2426.

2. The Securitization Theory has shown Significant Potentials to Incorporate Non-traditional Security Concerns within a Viable Framework. Buzan, B (1997), 'Re-thinking Security After the Cold War,' Cooperation and conflict, Decentralization' in R.D.Lipschutz(ed), on Security, Columbia University Press, New York; and Buzan, B., Waever, O, and de Wilde, J. (1997) security: A New Framework for Analysis, Lynne Rienner, Boulder, Co.

3. See for instance, Upadhyaya P., "Securitization Matrix in South Asia Bangladeshi Migrants as Enemy Alien", (Chapter 2), Anthony, Emmers and Acharya, (eds) *Understanding Non Traditional Security in Asia: Dilemma in Securitization* (Ashgate Pub., Hampshire, 2006)

4. See, Tilak D. Gupta, "Maoism in India Ideology, Programme and Armed Struggle", *Economic and Political Weekly*, July 22, 2006, pp. 3172-3176.

5. See Manoranjan Mahanty, "Challenges of Revolutionary Violance: The Naxalite Movement in Perspective", *Economic and Political Weelky*, July 22, 2006, pp. 3163-3168.

6. Sean DeBlieck, Why Mao? Maoist Insurgencies in India and Nepal, *Peace Conflict and Development*, 9, July 2006 at www. Peace Studies Journal.org.uk. P.V.Ramana, of the Observer Research Foundation Estimates the Armed Naxalities Around 9,000-10,000, with Access to About 6,500 Firearms. However such Statistics Naxlite Power, Since in most Places they are an Underground, hit-and-run Force.

7. See Prime Minister's Speech. *The Hindu*, New Delhi, April 14, 2006.

8. Cited by Praful Bidwai, *Meeting the Naxal Challenges*, October 11, 2005. Rediff.Com at in.rediff.com/news/2005/oct/11 bidwai.htm.

9. Sagar."The Spring and its Thunder", *Economic and Political Weekly*, July 22, 2006, pp. 3176-3178.

10. Some of the pro-Naxal Blogs are The Red Blood-http:/ struggle for survival.blogspot.com/Naxalnest- haxalnext.blogspot.com.ajad Hind-http://ajadhind.blogspot.com/Naxals in India-http://Naxals.blogspot/ Cuckoo's Call-http:/cuckooscall.blogspot.com/peoplesmarch-http:/ /peoplesmarch. wordpress.com/http://Naxalrevolution.blogspot.com

11. Annie Zaidi, Resisting the rebels. *Frontline*, 22 (21), Oct.08-21, 2005.

12. See Bela Bhatia, "On Armed Resistance", *Economic and Political Weekly*, July 22, 2006, pp. 3179-3183.

13. China Ready to Help India Crush Maoists (IANS), *The Hindustan Times*, 26 October 2005.

14. *The Hindu*, 26 May, 2006.

15. *The Hindu*, February 8, 2006.

16. *The 2005-06 Annual Report of the Union Ministry of Home Affairs*, p. 23.

17. *Hindustan Times*, September 9, 2006.

18. http:/www.india-defence.com/reprts/1997

19. ICC-ARSIPSO Seminar on National Seminar on National Security Internal & External Dimensions for India.http:/www.iicdelhi.in/ program/program_detail.asp?progid=1044&Cat.gld=1

20. Paritosh Chakravarty, "*Salwa Judum*: Adivasiyon Ka Singhnad," *Lokayat* (Hindi)31 July 2006, Delhi,.pp. 23-39 also see South Asia Intelligence Review, weekly Assessments & Briefings, Volume 4(7), August 29, 2005, http:/www.satp.org/satporgtp/sair/Archieves/ 4_7.hmt#assesment2

21. It has Displaced up to 40,000 Tribals who are now Huddled in All-equipped Government Relief Camps in the Worst Conceivable Conditions. see Ajaya Sahni, Look Who is Waving red Flag now, *The Indian Express*, 2 March 2006.

22. Between 31 January 2006 and June 2005 the Maoist Killed 95 Villagers who were involved in the *Salva Judam*.

23. See Ajaya K.Mehra, India's Nowhere Revolution: Riddles, Mysteries & Enigma, *Mainstream*, XLIV (34), August 12, 2006, Independence day Special, pp. 31-38.

24. Former Chief Justice of India, Venkatchaliah, M.N. (1997), *Proceedings of World Congress on Human Rights*, Institute for World Congress on Human Rights, India International Centre, New Delhi, 21-22 November.

2

PROBLEM OF NAXALISM IN GLOBALIZING INDIA

Amit Kumar Singh

Though Naxalite movement emerged a long time back,[1] yet in globalizing India it is acquiring a new fascia. Basically it is a movement launched by oppressed classes of the society. As we all know that this oppressed class took up arms against the age-old age oppression by landlords in the year of 1967. Since then it has passed through many different phases. Manoranjan Mohenty is focusing on these developments in his book "In Revolutionary Violence: A Study of the Maoist Movement in India".[2] He is advancing three propositions:

1. Naxalite movement is a pre-organized movement.
2. It practiced ideological parallelism to a large extent mechanically applying formulations of the Chinese revolution to contemporary India.
3. The strategy pursued by the Naxalites was a narrow construction of revolutionary strategy and was not always one of ideology and operation.

Earlier studies of naxalite movements in India have proved it very well that Dalits, Adivasis, and Small Farmers were the backbone of this movement.[3] Agrarian and anti-imperialist revolutions have contributed a lot in this context. The paper follows shall try to explore how much these movements are impressive for the indigenous development of the country and how much the process of globalization is creating new hindrance for them. Actually globalizers are trying to capture the agrarian fields, its production and distribution, in the similar manner as it was done by the feudalist class during the mid of the twentieth century. Difference is that earlier the exploiters were their own people and thus they have the idea of the nature of exploitation. Now they are open to be exploited by global exploiters i.e. World Bank, WTO, multi-national companies. Thus, they are still struggling for their survival. In fact nowadays they are struggling with two swords. First, the old landwards, who still exist along with their age old aspirations and expectations in interior parts of the areas where tribals are residing. And second, the globalizers who can go anywhere just like a new economic ghost! Thus it is very challenging, sad and pathetic for them to preserve their existence. Neither the national nor the international organization is assisting them in the real sense of the term. However it does mean to say that globalization is responsible for the problem of naxalism in India.

Though globalization is not proving its worthiness in the developing or under developing countries, yet positively it is contributing a lot. Skilfully we should learn how to utilize its resources. A thorough study of both of these facets may open our eyes with a new perspective. Let us have an extensive comparative analysis.

As we all know that Indian government adopted the policy of globalization in the year of 1991[4] while the problem of naxalism started in the year of 1967. Globalization is a centralized process as it is looking for one Global Village, contrary to that naxalism is a multi-faceted development. Every naxalite movement has its own cause of origin. It is possible that regionalism is playing central factor in one naxalite movement and in another a huge disparity between rich and poor is their main agenda of revolution. Thus naxalism is struggling for different causes unlike the global movement which is struggling for one universal cause. Further, one is concerned for the whole globe and other is bothering only for their people and region. Whatever the points of differentiations are there in their approaches and perspectives, the fact is that both of them are looking for the human and rational development of the society. Both of them are trying to cope up with the problems of contemporary world order. Thus ideally and positively both are good and healthy at their own sphere of action. However the only problem is that they are not assuming themselves as complementary to each other. Globalizers are trying to consume the resources of the tribal areas, thus consequently proving themselves as contradictory to local development.

In fact in this model of globalization there is a huge gap between rich and poor. There is a big disparity between modes of development. Service sector is developing rapidly but agricultural sector is totally ignored.[5] There is a consumer boom[6] in urban areas but in rural areas farmers are compelled to commit suicide[7]! Sensex is rising up but common people are struggling for their necessary basic needs. Mobile phones are becoming cheaper but the prices of food-grains are shooting up.[8] This is the negative aspect of globalization where common people are desperately looking for their space. Political scientist Ranjnee Kothatri also agrees with this preposition and agues that the process of globalization has created a very critical situation in India.[9] Following are some of those important points which need proper of discussion in this context:

1. The glorified status of the institution of state or government has declined. Now people are feeling that these institutions are no longer capable of solving their problems.[10] Now the old spirit of patriotism is not there. These days regionalism is more effective and powerful then nationalism.[11]

2. These regional movements and separation of the regions are main cause of concerns of the states. Clashes, conflicts and violence have become the order of the day and state is helpless and just seeing the whole scenario as a spectator.[12]

3. Not only this even the elites and the leaders of the nation find themselves unable to solve the problem. Political commitment and public accountability mean nothing these days. They have come into strong grip of the market forces which is shining around them.[13]

4. Religious, linguistic, social and ethnic factors are playing important role these days but unfortunately all of them have become commodity in this market oriented society. They are also getting influenced by power politics.[14]

5. Nation states are not trying to deal with the international or global problems and thus losing their relevance.

6. Multi-national companies are making their inroads and thus grass-root developments are getting affected.[15]

Eminent social scientists across the globe are accepting the fact that this process of globalization has weekend all the possibility of alternative ways and thus ruined the democratic spirit. This research paper shares its views with these scientists and uses the above assumptions while looking for the solution of the problem of naxalism in globalizing India.

The global experience of the process of globalization shows that it is far from being inclusive.[16] Even globalizers are assuming that it has enhanced the hitch between the rich and the poor.[17] Rich are becoming richer and poor poorer. The GDP of rich nations are sixty percent higher then the poor nations. 60% of world income is consuming by the rich nations and poor are bound to satisfy themselves with the rest.

According to Rurtor, during 1960s the income of the richer nations was thirty times more then the poor nations. This ratio increased in nineties by seventy four times. In 1820 this ratio was 3:1. It was10:1 in 1913. It became 35:1 in 1950 and in the year of 1991 it becomes 74:1.[18]

Even the economy of India is experiencing the same development. Rich are becoming richer and poor are becoming poorer. Number of billionaires is growing with the rate of 19.3%. Number of billionaires was 33,000 in the year of 2005. Moreover, India had 20,000 families whose annual income was more than 1 crore during 2001-02. By 2004 the numbers increased up to 53,000. And it is estimated that the number will cross 1,40,000 up to 2010.[19] It means on the one hand the number of billionaires is increasing and on the other hand, as records show the number of people living below the poverty line is also increasing with the same intensity!

Records of National Sample Survey (2004-2005) bring to light the fact that despite of the higher growth rate in post-reform period (1992-2005) the rate of decline in the poverty line is not more then that of the pre-reform period (1983-1993).[20]

Surprisingly though some of the states of the country are growing rapidly even then the poverty ratio is very high in these states. For instance in Orissa and Bihar this ratio is more then 30%, in Madhya Pradesh and Uttar Pradesh it is more about 40% and in Maharashtra, Tamil Nadu, Karnataka and West Bengal it is approx 25-30% during 2004-2005. It is very much alarming that during 2004-2005 in Orissa the poverty level was 47% and in Punjab it was only 8%. A cursory glance of these reports show that the situation of poor people in ruler areas is very pathetic.[21] Table 2.1 will help us in provoking our thoughts in this direction.

Table 2.1: Percentage of the distribution of poor people in States across the country.

STATE	*RURAL*			*URBAN*			*ALL*		
	1983	*1993-1994*	*2004-2005*	*1983*	*1993-1994*	*2004-2005*	*1983*	*1993-1994*	*2004-2005*
A.P.	4.70	3.49	2.81	7.54	9.35	6.89	5.31	4.89	3.88
Assam	2.89	3.86	2.54	0.66	0.37	0.18	2.41	3.03	1.92
Bihar	16.82	19.22	20.11	6.53	5.99	6.46	14.64	16.07	16.53
Gujarat	2.73	2.65	2.97	6..40	6.11	3.18	3.51	3.47	3.03
Haryana	0.93	1.45	0.96	1.16	1.08	1.37	0.98	1.37	1.07
H.P.	0.30	0.60	0.32	0.08	0.05	0.03	0.25	0.47	0.25
J & K	0.51	0.52	0.18	0.36	0.02	0.17	0.48	0.45	0.18
Karnataka	4.15	4.04	3.85	7.25	7.96	8.32	4.81	4.97	5.02
Kerala	3.22	2.43	134	3.56	2.66	2.22	3.29	2.48	157
M.P.	8.49	9.03	11.14	9.08	10.78	9.82	8.61	9.45	10.79
Maharashtra	7.71	7.91	7.97	13.97	15.52	17.08	9.04	9.71	10.36
Orissa	6.58	5.94	6.99	2.44	2.51	3.32	5.70	5.12	6.03
Punjab	0.73	0.84	0.71	1.72	1.05	0.66	0.94	0.89	0.70
Rajasthan	4.35	4.09	4.03	4.48	4.61	5.52	4.38	4.21	4.42
Tamil Nadu	7.56	4.94	3.47	11.83	11.08	13.48	8.47	6.40	6.11
U.P.	17.87	20.95	22.80	15.75	14.55	15.66	17.42	19.43	20.93
W.B.	10.47	8.04	7.80	7.17	6.13	5.62	9.77	7.59	7.23
All India	100.00	100.00	100.00	100.00	100.00	100.00	100.00	100.00	100.00

Source: Extracted form NSS 43rd, 50th and 61st round of consumer expenditure survey.

Table 2.1 reveals the fact that poor people are concentrated only in few states. Survey report of 1983 is saying that in four States i.e. M.P., Orissa, U.P. and Bihar 49% of poor people of the total population of the country were residing. This trend is continuously increasing, that is to say it was surveyed that 55% in 1993-94 and 61.6% in 2004-2005 are living in remote areas. Similarly percentage of the people residing in the urban areas in seven States– Bihar, Karnataka, MP, Maharashtra, Rajasthan, Tamil Nadu and UP are increasing from 61.6% in 1983 to 70% in 1993-97 and 76% in 2004-2005. Strangely most of these states are naxalite states. Though the percentage of the poor people is decreasing but there isn't nay major development in the condition of the very poor people in all these naxalite affected states. Bihar, UP, MP, Maharashtra and Orissa are the states where number of people are very high and still they are living at the verge of starvation.[22]

Further scientists are assuming that the regional disparity, which is the main cause of naxalite movement in India, is the outcome of the process of globalization. As Market forces within this process of globalization are not bothering for the balanced regional development; instead their main cause of concern is to make profit as much and as quickly as possible. Globalizers are not looking for legitimacy and accountability like state and its other institutions are apprehensive about it.[23] This can be seen in Table 2.2.

It is clear from Table 2.2 that Punjab has the highest per capita income all through and in Orissa it is lowest. In the context of annual average growth rate Bihar recorded the lowest however status of Karnataka is highest. Condition of Rajasthan, UP, Assam, MP is also very awful. On the whole the table shows that in this globalizing India things are not happening in pleasant and healthy manner. This is the reason why the voices of tribals are so strong here in these states. Government of India must consider the issue seriously and try to find out a practical solution at earliest possible manner.

Table 2.2: Per Capita Domestic Products (1993-1994)

STATES	*1990-1991 (in Rs.)*	*2000-2001 (in Rs.)*	*Annual Average Growth Rate (1990-91-2000-2001)*
Punjab	11779	15390	2.7
Maharashtra	10248	15172	4
Haryana	11125	14331	2.6
Gujarat	8788	12975	3.9
West Bengal	6013	9778	5
Karnataka	6629	11910	6
Kerala	6851	10712	4.6
Tamil Nadu	7872	12779	4.9
Andhra Pradesh	6873	9982	3.8
Backward States	6321	7003	-
Madhya Pradesh	5574	6157	1
Assam	5342	5770	1
Uttar Pradesh	6771	7937	0.8
Rajasthan	4300	5187	1.6
Orissa	4476	3345	1.9
Bihar	7321	10254	-2.8
All India Ratio Between Max. and Min. per capita NSDP	2.74	4.60	3.4

Source: Ministry of Finance Statistics (2001-2002).

Moreover, scientists like Dudley Seers[24] are challenging the process of *globalization in India*. They are arguing that at the one side India is emerging as a new global power but on its other side the seen of poor and unemployed people is very plight. They are putting forward some of very vibrant and relevant questions such as, "what has been happening to poverty?", "What has been happening to unemployment?" "What has been happening to equality?" so on and so forth. One can not ignore these questions. Even if the per capita income of rich people is becoming double, it can not be called as development because poor people are still suffering for their livelihood. An illustrative and in-depth study of the process of globalization in India will prove it very well that globalization is not going to solve this problem poverty, inequality and unemployment.

Unfortunately development in agrarian India means industrialization. One can say that as per the contemporary norms of development are concerned it is essentially required. We are also agreeing with the fact but government should take this issue very seriously and sensitively. Contrary to this our government does not have any healthy and rational alternative for rehabilitation of the displaced minorities.

Within the process of SEZ (special economic zone) governments' hypocritical and two-faced approach reflects towards the poor displaced people. After the introduction of the concept of SEZ as the vehicle of rapid industrialization, a mania has gripped several State governments to follow this route of rapid industrial progress. Big business houses – Indian as well as foreign multinationals – have made a beeline to get big proposal approved by the state. The CPI-M led West Bengal Government is the single state in which SEZS have become a major controversy. On the one extreme is Chief Minister Buddhadeb Bhattacharjee who showed unflinching determination to push the idea forward. On the other, there is Trinamual Congerss led by Mamta Banerjee who is sternly opposed to the manner in which the state government pushed its single-track agenda, more specially in Singur for the *Tata Small Car Project* and latter in Nandigram for the *Salim Chemicals Projects*. The chief argument employed to acquire land for big business houses was the Land Acquisition Act of 1894 which authorized the State Government to acquire land for "public purpose". It would be interest to understand the size of acreage which was proposed to be brought under SEZs in West Bengal.

According to the rough estimate prepared by D. Bandyopadhyay, former Secretary, Ruler Development, West Bengal who played a seminal role in implementing 'Operation Barga', it involves an acquisition of 1,40,000 acres in nine districts which include East Midnapur (37,297 acres), West Midnapur (26,134 acres), Howrah (26,500 acres), Darjeeling (25,200 acres), South 24 Parganas (13,318 acres), North 24-Parganas (5743 acres), Hooghly (6247 acres). Nadia (365 acres), and Jalpaiguri (161 acres). The State government took upon itself the responsibility to acquire land and hand it over to the big business houses for "public purpose". At persent, while land owners get 75 per cent of the value of land according to market price as compensation, bargadars get only 25 per cent. This is creating a lot of resentment as it is the bargadars who till and take 75 per cent to the owners. The government is considering a formula to increase compensation for bargadars to 75 per cent to bring them at par with landowners. In other words , compensation would be 150 per cent of value of land.

Meanwhile we witnessed over two thousand policemen along with CPI-M cadres on March 14, 2007 launched an unprecedented offensive, villagers were bitten, their houses were torched and a wave of ruthless suppression was unleashed to teach a lesson to those who were determinedly opposing land acquisition by the government of Nandigram. The police firing lead to the killing of 14 persons and hundreds were injured.[25]

The massive agitation in Singure and Nandigram in West Bengal had its repercussion in other States such as Orissa, Maharashtra, Haryana etc. the farmers are becoming increasing conscious about their exploitation by industrial houses and developers. Therefore, the attempt to deny land and protest against forced land acquisition. The Orissa government has informed POSCO that it will not use force to pursued farmers to vocate their lands for POSCO's Steel Project. The onus of acquiring land will henceforth be on POSCO and the POSCO officials have to inform people about rehabilitation and resettlement packagea and persuade farmers to give up their lands voluantarily. Maha Mumbai SEZ is to be built on 11,696 hectares or nearly 29,000 acres of land and this project will displace one lakh persons from 45 villages. Similary in Uttar Pradesh farmers are agitating against land acquisition by Relaince Group in Dadra. In Bastar *adivasis* are protesting against this policy of SEZ.[26]

Social activist and the leader of National Alliance of People's Movement Medha Patekar remarked, "The accelerated transfer of resources form agriculturists to real-estate developer, from common property to public property, from public sector to the private, from national domain to the foreign market, it paparazzi large section of its own citizens, poor to the middle classes, through deprivation of not just the livelihoods and resources, but also rights."[27]

Some of the critics are calling this policy of SEZ as nationwide loot.[28] Even Prime Minister Dr. Manmohan Singh admits it as mistake on the part of the government. He comments, "There is need for a human approach towards all those who have suffered for having lost livelihood through land acquisition for SEZ."[29]

These are not the new developments. From 1980 to 2003 about 8,47,000 hectares of forest land were occupied by the government for 10,118 project.[30] Moreover, the record of the rehabilitation process is very unhealthy. During 1947-2000 industrial projects in West Bengal took 47 lakh acres of land and affected 70 lakh people.[31] Thirty six lakh were displaced and 34 lakh deprived of livelihood without being physically relocated. A study shows 60 million displaced (DP)/project affected people (PAP) during 1947-2000 across the country. 10 % of these are coming form West Bengal, 20% are tribals, 30% are dalits and 20% are hailing form poor states.[32]

The scheduled tribes who constitute only 8.4 percentage of the total population of India are seriously facing threats. Since ages they have been denied to use the natural resources independently which is their natural rights. For instance, from

1980 to 2003 about 8,47,000 hectares of forest lands into industrial areas.[33] Thus, even in globalizing India a section of the voiceless society i.e. tribals, dalits, and poor farmers are seriously facing the threat and hence provoking the naxalite movements in different parts of the country.

As a consequence of this land acquisition bulk of the tribal people are bound to migrate. These migrated people are looking for help or assistance and Maoist know how to utilize this opportunity for their shake. A passage from north east through Jharkhand to Chhattisgarh at centre to Orissa and Andhra Pradesh in South is Maoist dominated area. It is called as Red Corridor, lashed with arms and ammunitions for their security purpose and to pressurize the government.[34] Official records are showing that they have widespread up to 100 districts around the country. They are concentrated in 76 districts of nine states where 25,000 members are involved there in militia operations. Earlier it concentrated only in 16 districts. Among 602 districts 106 districts are affected by naxalite movement some way or other. Within these 106 districts, 55 districts are badly affected. A parallel government of naxalite's is running in these districts.[35] The movement encompasses throughout 40% of the geographical area of the country and affecting 35% of the civilians in the country.[36] Goa, Pondichary, Andaman & Nichobar islands are the only states whom are not getting affected by naxalite movement at all. Let us have a look of the matter in Table 2.3.

Union Home Secretary *V.K. Duggle* reported that in the year of 2005 approximately 510 police stations have face naxalite attacks. Prime minister and other union ministers are accepting the truth with equal voice that naxalism is the biggest threat before the nation.[37] It is eye opening that the number of the blasts in Jharkhand and Chhattisgarh are more then the terrorist prone J&K.[38] just have a quick glance of Table 2.4.

Table 2.3: Statewise Naxalite Violence

STATES	*2002*		*2003*		*2004*		*2005*	
	INCIDENTS	*DEATHS*	*INCIDENTS*	*DEATHS*	*INCIDENTS*	*DEATHS*	*INCIDENTS*	*DEATHS*
A.P.	346	96	577	140	310	74	532	206
CHHATTISHGARH	304	55	257	74	352	83	380	165
JHARKHAND	353	157	342	117	379	169	308	118
BIHAR	239	117	250	128	323	171	183	94
MAHARASHTRA	83	29	75	31	84	15	95	53
ORISSA	68	11	49	15	35	8	42	14
M.P.	17	3	13	1	13	4	20	3
U.P.	20	6	13	8	15	26	10	1
WEST BENGAL	17	7	6	1	11	15	14	7
OTHER STATES	18	1	16	8	11	1	10	8
TOTAL	1465	482	1597	515	1533	566	1594	669

Source: Annual Report of Home Ministry, 2005-2006.

Table 2.4: Naxalite Attacks

	2002	*2003*	*2004*	*2005*
TOTAL EVENTS	1465	1597	1533	1594
CASUALITY OF CITIZEN	382	410	466	516
CASUALITY OF POLICE	100	105	100	153
DEATH OF NAXALITES	141	216	87	223

Source: Annual Report of Home Ministry, 2005-2006.

Poverty, unemployment, sense of deprivation and social exclusion are those cruxes of the problem which are provoking the naxalite movement in country. Bela Bhatia in his study says that the rural people are the leaders of these movements.[39] In these areas it is the well known fact only naxalite groups can protect their interests in the real sense of the term.[40] In Andhra Pradesh rural people are the real protectors of these movements. In Orissa about 22% of tribal people are the convener of the movement.[41] In Chatisgarh Bator, Konker and Dantewade are worst affected areas.[42] Similarly in Maharashtra every year 80% of both civilians and police personals are killing.[43]

Hence, the above illustrative and analytical study is revealing the fact, though India is becoming globalized by leaps and bound, however these globalizing forces are not equally fulfilling the aspirations of each and every region of the nation consequently we are badly facing this problem of naxalite movement in India. We must learn how to use the resources of the globalization so as to fulfil the expectations and requirements of the marginalized section of the country. In fact state must accept this reality that poor or marginalized are the real indicators of the development. Skillfully apathetic state should try to find out the strategy where both of them can play a cooperative role for the sake of human and rational development of the nation.

REFERENCES

1. Naxalite Movement Derives its Name from the Name of a Small Village Naxalbari Exists at the Tri-juncture of India, Nepal and [East] Pakistan.

2. Manoranjan Mohenty, 'Challenges of Revolutionary Violence', *Economic and Political Weekly*, July 22, 2006, p. 3163.

3. *Ibid.*, p. 3263.

4. See, Gurusharan Das, *India Undoubted* (Pengiun Books, New Delhi, 2001).

5. Jayanti Ghose, 'Whose India is Shining?', *Frontline*, Feb, 27, 2004, p. 89.

6. 'Consumer Boom: Then and Now', *Business Today*, Jan. 14, 2007, p. 168.

7. P. Sainath, 'It's Official Distress Up Suicide Appalling', *The Hindu*, Nov. 22, 2006, p. 11.

8. The Sensex in The Long Run, it is All Bull', *The Business World*, Jan. 1, 2007, pp. 92-93.

9. Rural India Lives on Rs. 18/day', *The Times of India*, Dec. 29, 2006, p. 1.

10. Rajani Kothari, *Janta se Darte Abhijan Aur Kamjoor Hota Rastra Rajya'* in Abhay Kumar Dubey (ed.) *Bharat Ka Bhoomandalikaran* (Vani Prakashan, New Delhi, 2003) p. 76.

11. Dhiru Bhai Seth, *Bajaronmookh Ya Sahbhage Looktantra*, p. 108.

12. Rajani Kothari, p. 76.

13. Dhiru Bhai Seth, p. 109.

14. Rajani Kothari, p.77.

15. *Ibid.*

16. Jagadish Bhagavati does not Agree with this Assumption, See *In Defense of Globalization*, p. 21.

17. Joseph Stiglitz, *Globalization and its Discontent* (Penguin, New Delhi, 2002) p. 24.

18. N. Murphy Caring, 'Political Consequences of the New Inequality', *International Studies Quarterly*, 2001, No. 45, p. 348.

19. David Doller and Arat Karry, 'Spreading the Wealth', *Foreign Affairs*, Jan-Feb, 2002, 81(1), 120-133, p. 121.
20. S. Mahendra Dev, C. Ravi, 'Poverty and Inequality: All India and States 1983-2005', *Economic and Political Weekly*, (Feb. 10, 2007) p. 512.
21. *India Today*, Jan. 3, 2005.
22. Ruddar Dutta, K.P.M. Sundaram, *Indian Economy* (S.Chand, New Delhi) p. 473.
23. Baldev Raj Nayar, *The Geopolitics of Globalisatics of Globalisation, The Consequences for Development* (Oxford, New Delhi, 2005) p. 16.5187
24. Dudley Seers, "The Meaning of Development", *International Development Review*, Vol. 11, No. 4.
25. *Mainstream*, Vol. XLV, No. 15, New Delhi, March 31, 2007, pp. 11-16.
26. 'Security At Tata Project Site in Baster Tightened', *The Times of India*, March 2, 2007, p. 5.
27. *Business and Economy*, Feb. 23-March 8, 2007, p. 81.
28. *'SEZ Ka Virodh'*, The Sunday India, Jan 28, 2007, p. 8.
29. PM Hints At SEZ relook, *The Times of India*, March 9, 2007, p. 114.
30. Ashis Kothari, op. cit., p. 14.
31. Fernandes Walter, Not A People's State, *The Times of India*, Dec. 13, 2006, p. 14.
32. *Ibid.*, p. 14.
33. Maoist blamed for JMM, MP, *The Times of India*, March 7, 2007, p. 16.
34. Venkitesh Ramkrishna, 'The Naxalite Challenges', *Frontline*, Oct. 21, 2005, p. 4.
35. R.K. Bhonsle, 'An Integrated Strategy', *Yojana*, Feb. 2007, p. 33.
36. *The Hindu*, April 15, 2006.
37. K. Srinivas Readdy, 'Naxal Government Rethinking Strategies', *The Hindu*, Dec. 13, 2006, p. 11.
38. 'Killing with Impurity', *The Hindu*, March 6, 2007, p. 10.

39. Bela Bhatia, *Adhunikta ke Aainey main Dalit*, Vani Prakashan, (New Delhi 2002) p. 317.

40. *Ibid.*, p. 318.

41. Prafulla Das, 'In A State of Fear', *Frontline*, Oct. 21, 2005, p. 13.

42. Nadini Sundar, 'Baster Maoism and Salwa Judum', *Economic and Political Weekly*, July 22, 2006, p. 3138. Also see, The Outrage in Chhatisgarh, The Hindu, March 17, 2007, p. 10.

43. Dionee Bunsha, 'Gurilla Zone', *Frontline*, Oct 21, 2005, p. 16.

3

NAXALISM IN INDIA
QUEST FOR GOOD GOVERNANCE

Dr. Alka R. Gupta

The debate over the issue that whether Naxalism is an expression of economic-injustice or a product created due to an absence of law and order is in air now everywhere.But there is no utility to linger on such debate. Rather it is high time to trace the root causes of the issue and draft a national policy for its eradication entirely. Naxal violence has claimed hundreds of lives in the recent past and turned out as a serious national security problem. Now the Naxal issue has been labeled as India's biggest internal security problem and this label carries no ifs or buts in general terms. Naxalism can be identified as a particular set of terrorism at the internal level of the country. If terrorism is fundamentally an attack on the state and described as an act of violence, committed against innocent people to create fear, with an underlying political motive then this meaning contains same implications almost for the Naxalism. The total structure of Naxalism today represents an institutional form of terrorism with guerrillas capable of isolated large scale military operations. Although it is a different thing to be analyzed that Naxal movement was launched initially to safeguard innocent and poor people's interests but later on it has diverted from its original aim. Indeed today Naxalism is another name for threatening common people, hampering peace and destroying law and order in more than half states of the country.

NAXALISM: IDEOLOGICAL BACKGROUND

Originally Naxalism is based on the theory of class-struggle of Karl Marx. Actually long back in China Mao tse-tung established the socialism through democratic revolution with a huge mass support. Theoretically he applied Marxism and Leninism in the communist movement to the needs of an overwhelmingly agricultural and still traditional society. Indian Naxalites accept Maoism (It is usually understood as an anti-bureaucratic form of Marxism that places its faith in the radical zeal of the masses) at the ideological level but their strategies and method of revolt is unlike from Maoist theory. In fact, Naxalism in India is an ideological, political and economic struggle to establish economic, social and political equality and abolish any kind of exploitation in the society.

The emergence of peasant resistance by santhal tribals in a village of Naxalbari in West Bengal in the decade of 1960 later on known as Naxalites' movement in 1967. The Naxalbari uprising of March 1967 saw the implementation of Charu Majumdar's vision of revolution "Expand anywhere and everywhere". Charu majumdar who led the movement is known as the father of Naxalism. The ultra-leftist ideology took a concrete shape at May 1968 meeting of *All India Coordination Committee of Communist Revolutionaries* (AICCCR) which represented revolutionaries from seven states of Tamil Nadu, Kerala, UP, Bihar, Karnataka, Orissa and West Bengal. In 1969, Communist Party (Marxist-Leninist) was formed under the leadership of Charu Majumdar. It argued that democracy in India was a sham and decided to base Indian revolution on protracted guerrilla warfare on the lines of Chinese Model. There were three announced mottos of Naxal movement: *First* to provide the land right to the peasants, *second* to abolish the foreign capital power and *third* to struggle against the class and caste. However, the famous 1970 programme of CPI (ML) projected an understanding that a strong worker-peasant alliance and effective implementation of Mao's theory can help revolutionaries to defeat powerful enemies like big landlords, bureaucrats, capitalists and government, which is a "lackey of US imperialism and Soviet Social imperialism".

During the period from the sixties to seventies, the Naxal movement was crushed heavily and then the groups believing Maoist theory disintegrated and many streams created. Such as Kondapalli Seetharamaiah formed the Peoples War (PW) Group in Andhra Pradesh in 1980 and Kanhai Chatterzi formed Maoist Communist Center. The "rebellion" was crushed but the saga of terror and violence that entailed continues in different streams despite severe crackdown on them over decades.

NATURE

The Naxal movement in India is an area of increased concern in terms of intensity of violence, militarization, linkages with secessionist groups, and efforts to generate mass support. The Naxalites operate in a vacuum created due to an absence of administrative and political institutions; thereby the exploited segments of the population seek an alternative system of governance through the barrel of gun. The Indian Prime Minister, Manmohan Singh, during chairing the meeting of chief ministers of Naxal-infested states described the problem as the biggest internal security challenge. While L K Advani branded it as 'the worst enemy of the Indian dream'.

In the beginning the Naxal movement was launched to safeguard the interests of the economically underprivileged people who had to bear the atrocities of the rich landlords following strong genuine reasons but with the passage of time the movement seems to have converted into an anti-social problem. How can Naxalism provide social equality by indulging in kidnapping, killing of police personnel and thereby creating fear and unrest in general public? It is agreed that Naxal movement gets its strength from being the champion of the cause of poor and oppressed, but violence in society will always be dealt with punishment by the state machinery.

Investigations reveal that Naxalites are involved in illicit narcotic trade and smuggling of counterfeit Indian currency. The Naxalites have a very well-knit organizational structure and have a pan-India strategy. They aim to control the economic resources of the region and operate in areas rich in natural resources like minerals, *tendu patta, katha* trees, etc. Besides terrorizing the local populace and traders, the Naxalites have also resorted to extortion. The Naxalites leadership continues to pursue its plan to wage a protracted people's war through the armed struggle to capture political power. They seem to lay greater focus on organizing along military lines. Their constant effort is to upgrade their weaponry. Regular cadre recruitment is carried out. And now schools are being the latest focus of attention. Their aim here is to create '*bal-dasta*', or child squads.

The Maoist movement in India can presently be classified into three phases – organisation phase, guerrilla warfare phase and mobile warfare phase. In the Organisation stage, Maoist cadres concentrate on building up agitations on people's issues and violence is extremely selective (strategic defensive). In the guerrilla phase, the revolutionaries see themselves to be on an equal footing with the state and fight for area domination. This is the stage where violence reaches a crescendo, as the rebels use shoot-and-scoot attacks on security forces (strategic stalemate). The mobile warfare phase is one where the rebels control the area and the security forces are forced to be on permanent guard (strategic offensive).

It is difficult to demarcate the areas state-wise, as there is bound to be a large overlap among the three phases. However, the *Left Wing Extrimist* (LWE) movement in the Bastar forest areas of Chhattisgarsh is undoubtedly in the mobile warfare stage, where revolutionaries and people's militia clearly have an upper hand over the security forces.

While the guerrilla phase can be seen in parts of Andhra Pradesh, Bihar, Jharkhand, Maharashtra, Orissa and West Bengal, the organization stage is visible in Madhya Pradesh, Uttar Pradesh, Karnataka, Haryana, Tamil Nadu, Kerala and Uttarakhand and parts of Andhra.

In 1971 Naxal movement was limited only in four states but today the picture is very grim. Almost 225 districts of 16 states of the country are directly affected from it. 8,695 police station areas are affected by Naxalism. There are about 9,500 Naxalites spread across these affected states. The Naxal area in the country bas been expanded more than the terrorist–separatist movement affected area. According to the government data, if we add all terrorist rebels of Jammu and Kashmir, Punjab and North-East states then its impact area is 11.09% of the country and 4.51% of the population. While almost 40% area and 35% population of the country is under the Naxal grip.

The area where Naxalites occupy the in depth impact over there they run their parallel government. Naxalites provides emancipation to poor, oppressed class and tribal from Police exploitation. They arrange interest-less loan to them. Not only this had they set public court to sort out their local problems and give the lands of landlords to the farming peasants.

The Naxalite movement is mostly active in the tribal areas spreading from Bihar to Andhra Pradesh and Maharashtra, and also covering parts of Jharkhand, Madhya Pradesh, Chhattisgarh, Orissa, Tamil Nadu and Karnataka. This spread is linked only to the inaccessible hilly terrain of these regions, but a conscious decision by the Naxalites to take up the issues affecting the tribal people the most exploited segment of the society. India's development process has led to commercialization of forest resources, reducing the traditional access to forest capital. Alienation of tribal land to non-tribal has been a steady trend despite legal restrictions.

Mining-based industries and the construction of large dams have caused extensive displacement of the tribals, besides destroying their natural environment. A central Naxalite agenda is for tribal self-determination, asserting the rights of the tribal over local resources.

Table 3.1: Summary of Naxal *Violence in 2006*

2006	*Incidents*	*Security Killed*	*Civilian Killed*
Andhra Pradesh	183	10	37
Bihar	107	5	40
Chhattisgarh	715	84	304
Jharkhand	310	43	81
Orissa	44	4	5
Maharashtra	98	3	39
Madhya Pradesh	6	–	1
West Bengal	23	8	9
Uttar Pradesh	11	–	5
Karnataka	10	–	–
Kerala	2	–	–
Total	1509	157	521

Source: www.naxalwatch.com

Nowhere is this conflict more acute than in the dense forests of southern Chhattisgarh state, the scene of violent land disputes and social clashes. In the past year an anti-Naxal movement launched in Bastar region of Chhattisgarh, known as *Salva Judum* (Peace March). *Salva Judum* activists mobilized villagers and tribals against Naxalites through various rallies and meetings. In actual this is a peaceful and voluntary movement by local people. Salwa Judum envisaged close coordination between the security forces and the local people but it soon degenerated into a private militia that behaved in much the same manner as the naxalites, killing to settle old scores in their villages, looting and perpetrating atrocities on those who opposed them. The government's strategy, under the Salwa Judum campaign, of picking up able-bodied local men, giving them arms training and inducting them as Special Police Officers (SPOs) to assist the security forces in anti-naxal operations also backfired.Indeed, people have found themselves caught between the Salwa Judum and the naxals charged up to neutralise the campaign. The naxals changed their strategy of targeting security forces or government officials and started killing tribal people in villages where residents participated in the Salwa Judum's activities. This should be protected from the brutal suppression of Naxalites, although this is gaining popularity and space among the common

REASONS

It is true that Naxalites got inspiration for their growth from China but no doubt India's social, political and economic conditions also forced them to develop. After the independence various programmes introduced for the rural area development. But due to feudal nature of the authority, complex rules and regulations, corruption, administrative dullness and the lack of general awareness, the real benefit of development process limited within few selfish groups and people. The land reforms could not implement effectively. The very fact that land reform as a state objective has disappeared from Indian policy-making in the age of economic liberalization. The announced targets during Five-Year Plans achieved to the very limited extent. Moreover, the policies of LPG (Liberalization, Privatization and Globalization) initiated in 1991 acknowledged the social-economic inequality as the binding part of development process. The state's anti-poverty programmes such as the NDA's Food-for-Work or the UPA's recently established Employment *Guarantee Programme* hardly meet the basic demand for land rights in rural India. The rise of backward castes to power in Bihar, Uttar Pradesh and elsewhere, even though it may have democratized certain aspects of the polity, has had the paradoxical effect of freezing land relations. All these have kept the Naxal agenda alive.

COMPACT REVULUTIONARY ZONE (CRZ)

The South *Asian Maoists Organizations* carved out a *Compact Revolutionary Zone* (CRZ) or what is called a "Red Corridor of armed struggle" spreading from Nepal through Bihar up to the Dandakarnaya region of Andhra Pradesh. These areas are home to various tribes who depend on the forest for their livelihood. As these tribal communities are heavily dependent on agriculture, the Naxalites have devised the idea of digging lakes, which could be used for irrigation and fish breeding. This idea laid the foundation of *Janatana Sarkar* or people's government. It is an alternative form of governance established by the Naxalites. A strong bond binds the Naxalites to the local people. This bond is fostered through monthly village meetings that discuss common problems and needs. To realize the plan of Red Corridor the Naxalites began to group up with other splinter groups and to intensify the mass contact programme. Subsequently the merger of the CPML (*Communist Party Marxist-Leninist*-PW (People's War) and MCCI (Maoist communist Center of India) into the CPI (Communist Party of India (Maoists)) in September 2004 took place. Of the two groups, the MCCI was known for its brutal methods, and the PW was considered to be moderate. The recent (January-February 2007) 9th Party Congress by CPI (Maoist) signals another phase in the cycle of Maoist insurgencies in India. The Naxal leadership views this as a grand success since the Maoists were holding a unity congress after a gap of 36 years - their 8th Congress was held in 1970. The Maoists claim that the Congress resolved the disputed political issues in the Party through lively, democratic and comradely debate and discussion. This Maoist claim hints at the new developments within the politics of Naxalism. It is also significant for the admission of the existence of 'inter-organizational' and 'intra-organizational' conflict within the political gamut of CPI (Maoist).

INTERNATIONAL SUPPORT BASE

Since the decade of 1980 Indian Naxalites intensified their efforts to obtain the international support besides establishing the contact and coordination with other countries' terrorist organizations having similar lines.The first signs of contact between the Maoists of the neighboring countries was reportedly registered during 1989-1990, when the two groups started collaborating in order to expand their area of influence. Subsequently, they began the process of building up what is now known as the Revolutionary Corridor extending from Nepal across six Indian States, including Bihar, Chhattisgarh, Jharkhand, Andhra Pradesh, Orissa and Madhya Pradesh. This area came to be called the Compact Revolutionary Zone (CRZ). The establishment of the CRZ provided a wider platform to the Nepalese and Indian left-wing extremist organizations to strengthen their base of operations in the two countries.In 1996 Indian Naxalites participated in the International Conference conducted by Workers Party of Belgium. There were almost sixty organizations of forty countries including Philippines, Germany, Peru, Turkey, Japan, Mexico, Spain, Russia gathered and participated.

The more radical groups in South Asia, including both the PWG and the Nepalese Maoists, are members of the '*Revolutionary Internationalist Movement*' (RIM). In July 2001, about 10 Extrimist Left Wing (Maoist) groups in South Asia formed the *Coordination Committee of Maoist Parties and Organization of South* Asia (CCOMPOSA) known as the first international coalition of Red terror in which the Nepalese Maoists, Maoist Communist Centre (MCC), PWG, Purbo Banglar Movement (Bangladesh), Communist Party of Ceylon (Sri Lanka) and other Indian left-wing extremist parties became members.

The Naxalites have cultivated links with Nepali Maoists, LTTE and even the ISI. From them they get sophisticated weapons and knowledge about improvised explosive devices along with training by the LTTE. These groups are also getting financial support from anti-India forces. There is also some reportage about the Nepalese Maoists' links with insurgent groups active in India's Northeast like United Liberation Front of Assam (ULFA), Kamtapur Liberation Organisation (KLO), Gurkha National Liberation Front (GNLF) and Gurkha Liberation Organisation (GLO).

THE GOVERNMENT STRATEGY

The government has defined a policy to combat Naxalism by simultaneously addressing issues pertaining to politics, security, development and public perception management. The *Ministry of Home Affairs Report of 2005-06* delineates three priority areas to deal with the Naxal menace. These are: local capacity building of the affected states in terms of intelligence gathering and training police forces for effective military action; making the administrative machinery more responsive, transparent and sensitive for effectively dealing with public grievances; and encouraging peace dialogues between the affected states and the Naxal groups. As per the need for economic assistance, the Ministry has administered three schemes to strengthen the security apparatus at the state level-*Security Related Expenditure* (SRE), Police Modernization, and *Backward District Initiative* (BDI). Where the first two are focused on combating the Naxal threat from a military perspective, the third addresses the problem through a development paradigm. As per the latest data provided in the report (2006), an advance of Rs. 20 crore has been released to the Naxal-affected states. Regarding the police modernization scheme (in terms of modern weaponry, mobility, communications equipment and training infrastructure), the Central Government has released Rs. 3,065.62 crore to the Naxal affected areas. These areas have also been sanctioned India Reserve Battalions, to not only supplement the security apparatus but also provide employment to the youth in these areas. As far as the initiatives regarding integrated development of the affected regions are concerned, under the scheme of Backward District Initiative, a total sum of Rs. 2,475 crore for the Naxal-affected areas have been sanctioned.

At 30 July 2005 meeting of the Chief Ministers and the Directors Generals of Police from the nine Naxalites-affected states agreed to set up a task force to launch joint operations. A policy of "Zero Tolerance" towards the Maoists was announced. The Tamil Nadu government had already banned the Maoist Party on 12 July, and the Karnataka government had also earlier launched joint operations with the Andhra police. The Andhra government's decision to have a special tribal battalion of some 1,200 men, a 'Girijan Greyhound" to fight the Naxalites is indicative of the approach guiding the present policy.

The government programmes of tribal development have ended up creating new elite in the tribal areas even as increased poverty leads to massive out-migration. The recent bill for safeguarding land rights, introduced by the UPA, has been a case of too little, too late. The extension of the Panchayati Raj programme to tribal areas, giving greater power to the tribal village assembly is a modest measure in the right direction, but unless structural measures are undertaken to restore rights over land and forest, the Panchayati Raj structures will continue to be manipulated by local elites.

The Union government on March 13, 2006 tabled the status report on the problems of Naxlalism in India. Here, the government accepts that the Naxalite movement continues to persist in terms of spatial spread, intensity of violence, militarization and consolidation, ominous linkages with subversive/secessionist groups and increased efforts to elicit mass support. While tabling this report the ex-Union Home Minister Shivraj Patil outlined the 14-point strategy to deal with the Naxal problems in India. The report deals in following policy matters mainly:

1. He conceded that naxalism is not merely a law and order problem, therefore the Government should address this menace simultaneously on political security, development and public perception management fronts in a holistic manner.

2. Acknowledging naxalism as an inter-state problem, the report says that the states will have to adopt a collective approach and pursue a coordinated response to counter it.
3. The report also emphasizes that the states need to improve police response and pursue effective and sustained police action against naxalites and their infrastructure individually and jointly.
4. The Union government categorically said in the report that there would be no peace dialogue by the affected states with the naxal groups unless the latter agree to give up violence and arms.
5. Outlining the importance of meaningful political involvement of the affected populace in the mainstream politics the report asks the political parties to strengthen their cadre base in naxsal affected areas so that the potential youth there can be weaned away from the path of naxal ideology.
6. The report asks to adopt an approach with special focus on accelerated sociw-economic development of the backward areas by ensuring the regular involvement of NGOs, intelligentsia, civil liberties groups etc. to minimize over ground support for the naxalite ideology and activity in the affected areas.
7. The government now focuses now on the efficient use of the Mass media to highlight the futility of naxal violence and loss of life and property caused by it and developmental schemes of the Government in the affected areas so as to restore people's faith and confidence in the Government machinery.
8. The report also says that there is an urgent need of according higher priority by the state government to the faster socio-economic development in the affected areas within the territory of the respective states. The focus areas should be to distribute land to the landless poor as part of the speedy

implementation of the land reforms, ensure development of physical infrastructure like roads, communication, power etc. and provide employment opportunities to the youth in these areas.

The Ministry of Home affairs has requested all the Naxal affected states to implement the "SURRENDER-CUM-REHABILITATION" scheme for the Naxalites who want to shun and join in the majority interest of the mainstream Government. For this scheem centre has provided assistance to the state governments. Recently, the Jharkhand government has offered monthly allowance of Rs. 2000, life insurence worth Rs. 10 lakh, vocational training for two years, one acre agri-land and free education to the Naxalites and their families.

The Centre has declared that it would launch a joint venture in the Naxal affected states but these steps are being perceived merely as a 'fire-fighting' operation. No doubt, the Naxal menace is acquiring dangerous proportions continuously. Hence, there is an urgent need to draft a uniform policy and a national agenda to fight against Naxalism otherwise it would be too late even to think for such policy.

GLOBALIZATION

During the 1990s, Indian politics and economy saw major upheavals linked to globalization. The processes of privatization of public enterprises and retrenchment of workers have continued unabated in the recent years. While the ruling parties, the BJP and the Congress, were fully committed to the agenda of globalization, the CPI and CPI-M tried to keep the critique alive on behalf of workers, the lower middle classes and the rural poor who suffered tremendously and largely silently under the process of economic reforms. But the main resistance to globalization was put forth by the Naxalites, which has considered the stress on anti-imperialism paramount at a time of growing collaboration between the government of India and the US government. There is a view in a section of observers that the current multi-pronged initiative against Naxalites is linked to the efforts to "ensure safe passage" to liberalization and globalization policies in large parts of rural India. If that is the case, the battle between Naxalites and the state apparatus will acquire more intense proportions in the days to come.

Basically Naxalism is a socio-economic development problem. Successive governments had failed to address the root cause of the problem and this failure has resulted in the problem of law and order and threatening the very fabric of a civilized society. Unless the root cause is examined and remedial steps taken to set them right, there is no escape from the recurring bloody incidents. More than the lack of development, Naxalism is thriving due to a *"crisis of governance"* where the political will to tackle the menace is "lacking". The oft-given excuse of underdevelopment to explain the reason for growing insurgency is nothing but an excuse for inaction.

An analytical view of the affected areas would reveal common characteristics of failure of governance and the processes of nation building summarized as given below:

- Dependence of a majority of the people on agricultural at the subsistence level, a primitive form of surviving nature" bounty, with no human intervention in the form of planned farming, soil replacement, regeneration and market dictated sowing patterns.
- Extractive mining, forestry and allied produce, which are highly exploitative, remain the only other economic activity.
- Modernization in terms of education, health care and secondary employment in blue and white collar jobs or services are virtually non existent.
- Apathy of the administration to the needs of the people on the plea of non intervention in tribal culture, customs and traditions and stasis as well as hubris of bureaucratic governance.

- Lack of empathy of the political class which in a modern system of administration and legislative functioning tends to gravitate away from the grassroots

No doubt we lack effective governance today. Chandrababu Naidu, an ex-Chief Minister had been talking about *Smart Governance:* simple, moral, accountable, responsive and transparent government. Unfortunately it is contrary. There are enormous delays. There are criticisms about the ancient laws which clutter out system and thereby lead to red tape. The role of minister is to decide policies while bureaucracy is to implement those. But we find that the political leadership takes more interest in administrative actions like transfers and postings and policy is generally neglected.

Another reason for delay is the plethora of rules and regulations which are like cancer cells. They don't know when to die. As a result, obsolete rules and proceedings create administrative bolltenecks. Concept of Sunset principle could be an option as in the United States' laws so that no rule or regulation should be on the statute book forever and ever. The laws may have a lifetime of five or ten years at the end of which it would automatically lapse unless, it is consciously reviewed and extended which is not so India.

The level of governance at the moment needs tremendous improvement. Out of the nearly 600 districts of India, in about 240 districts, the law and order situation is not satisfactory according to a Home Ministry. We face from time to time the anti-Indian activities of foreign agencies like the ISI. Moreover Naxalism poses threat to general people in drastic manner.

THE SEARCH FOR SOLUTION

The current scenario in India reflects the wrong application of counter-strategies in almost all the states. The root cause of this is that policy-makers primarily focus on tackling the Maoist problem on a military plane and blindly ask the affected states to follow examples like the Andhra

Pradesh model without correcting the mistakes committed by the state. The social and economic changes are taking place widely as well as the liberalization, privatization and globalization programmes are in running mode are not being considered when similar strategies are proposed elsewhere. The political leadership is neither ready nor willing to answer the questions raised by the Maoists in regard of people's issues at large – be it what they see as 'gross injustice' meted out to the tribal population in respect of setting up heavy industries in forest areas, or displacement of people owing to industrial activity. Andhra Pradesh is the best example that can be cited for scaling down revolutionary activity. It was in the mobile warfare stage with the People's Liberation Guerrilla Army almost running a parallel government in some areas, when the state managed to crush mass organization activity through the use of 'civil vigilante' groups it had carefully encouraged. Groups of surrendered Naxalites under the names of 'Cobras' and 'Tigers', covertly supported by the police, resorted to killing leaders of mass organizations and civil rights activists. The 'fear psychoses' created among the workers of these organizations, which have ideological similarities with the naxalites, has forced them into silence. The success of the Andhra Pradesh strategy is now sought to be replicated in other naxal-affected.

Ideally, governments should base their response on a correct assessment of the field level situation. Any inconsistent response would only further alienate people and is bound to be counterproductive.

A key element of the solution enunciated by the Indian Prime Minister Manmohan Singh was to 'walk-on-two-legs', wherein the military and development solutions are to be implemented simultaneously. On many an occasion, chief ministers of naxalism-affected states have also spoken on similar lines–that of tackling the problem on a socioeconomic plane.

Although in our Constitution Articles 36 to 51 outline an important part of the framers' vision for good governance administration, which unfortunately was given scant regard to for many years by the state, either because of economic limitations or by deliberate political choice.

In early June 2008 the recent realeased report of *the Planning Commission's Expert Committee on* the causes of 'Discontent, Unrest and Extremism' has put the blame on the state for the growth of the movement. Providing statistics of 125 districts from the Naxal-affected States, the committee finds out that the state bureaucracy has pitiably failed in delivering good governance in these areas.

GOOD GOVERNANCE

Nowadays the two terms "governance" and "good governance" have become very fashionable during any talk concerning development or nation-building. Bad governance is frequently considered as one of the root causes of all evils within societies. The concept of "governance" is not new. It is as old as human civilization. In Simple manner "governance" stands for: the process of decision-making and its implementation. Hereby, public institutions conduct public affairs, manage public resources, and guarantee the realization of public rights. Governance can be used in several contexts such as corporate governance, international governance, national governance and local governance.

Government is one of the actors in governance. Other actors involved in governance vary according to their level. In rural areas, for example, other actors may include influential land lords, associations of peasant farmers, cooperatives, NGOs, research institutes, religious leaders, finance institutions political parties, the military etc. The situation in urban areas is much more complex. All actors other than government and the military are grouped together as part of the "civil society".

The term *Good Governance* has been used for the first time by the *United Nations Development Programme* (UNDP) in its 2004 policy document.It focusses on the initiative and capacities to ensure human development that gives priority to the poor, advances women, sustains the environment and creates needed opportunities for employment and other livelihoods.

Good governance prescribes an ideal which is difficult to achieve in its totality. However, to ensure sustainable human development, actions must be taken to work towards this ideal. At the best it may be defined that good governance is associated with efficient, effective and economic administration particularly citizen-friendly, citizen-caring and transparent administration in a democratic framework.The governing process must be just,reasonable,fair and empathetic. Further it must be kept in mind that good governance is not simple something that governments can achieve or do by themselves. Instead, it depends on the co-operation and involvement of a large number of citizens and organisations. Major donors and international financial institutions, like the *IMF* or *World Bank*, is increasingly basing their *aid* and loans on the condition that reforms ensuring *good governance* are undertaken.

Good governance has eight major characteristics. It is participatory, consensus oriented, accountable, transparent, responsive, effective and efficient, equitable and inclusive and follows the rule of law. It assures that corruption is minimized, the views of minorities are taken into account and that the voices of the most vulnerable in society are heard in decision-making. It is also responsive to the present and future needs of society.

PARTICIPATION

Participation by both men and women is a key cornerstone of good governance. Participation could be either direct or through legitimate intermediate institutions or representatives. It is important to point out that representative democracy does not necessarily mean that the concerns of the most vulnerable in society would be taken into consideration in decision making. Participation needs to be informed and organized. This means freedom of association and expression on the one hand and an organized civil society on the other hand.Till date the actors of Naxalism have been deprived from the participation in the government in real terms. So it is very pertinent to give them a fair chance to be an active participant in the process of governance and make them realize that their role in the nation building is unavoidable and compulsory. Recently the Nepali citizen society can hope for peace and development after providing space to Maoists in their government structure because they have been the root cause for Nepal insurgency and backwardness. So it is high time for getting ready the oppressed class and deprived class to play the civil role after participating directly or indirectly in the governance and ensure civic culture in the country. Expansion of governance particularly at the grass root level is the key to normalize the situations.

Fig. 3.2: Eight characteristics of Good Governance

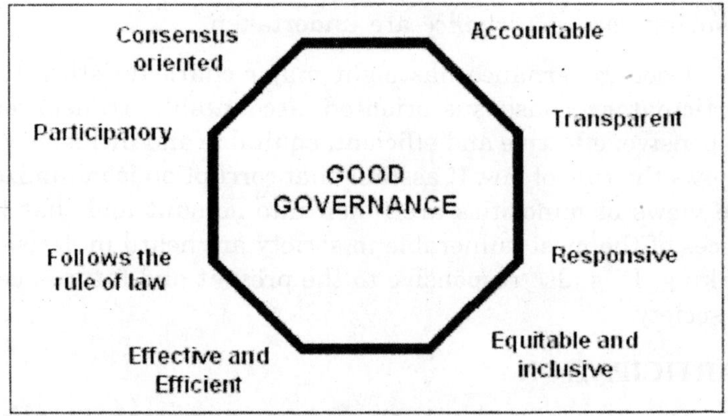

Source: UNESCP 2007.

RULE OF LAW

Good governance requires fair legal frameworks that are enforced impartially. It also requires full protection of human rights, particularly those of minorities. Impartial enforcement of laws requires an independent judiciary and an impartial and incorruptible police force. Policing is a principal facet for restoring the normalcy. A well- trained, sensitive, citizen-friendly but firm police force is a necessary element of it. Approach to Naxal problem should be with a social outlook within the framework of law. It can be termed as Social Policing which entails the synergy between the citizen and the Policemen through mutual respect thereby targeting Police activity towards hard core crime rather than marginal activities.

TRANSPARENCY

Transparency means that decisions taken and their enforcement are done in a manner that follows rules and regulations. It also means that information is freely available and directly accessible to those who will be affected by such decisions and their enforcement. Information needs to be leveraged as a core strategy for monitoring implementation. Recently passed the bill of Right to Information may be helpful in real terms for every citizen to access the latest information about the on-going progress of government. Here it is noted that enough information should be provided and that should be in easily understandable forms. Media can play a vital role to spread the awareness among the common mass.

RESPONSIVENESS

Good governance requires that institutions and processes try to serve all stakeholders within a reasonable timeframe. This is one of the great tragedies of Indian government. Fortunately we are very fine (paper) engineers to craft attractive and ambitious plans, schemes and projects for the cause of poverty, unemployment, health or land reforms but on the ground we fail to deliver the targets to the needed people. The *Asian Centre for Human Rights* (ACHR) in July 2007 pointed out that there has been no dearth of development schemes in India but the implementation of such schemes perennially remained problematic and implementation of the schemes in the naxalite-affected areas almost came to virtual halt because of the increased conflict. An estimated Rs. 6,

500 crores meant for implementation of the National Rural Employment Guarantee Programme (NREGP) were not spent during 2005-2006 and Rs. 1, 522.90 crores for development of the tribals could not be released by the Ministry of Tribal Affairs to various State governments by the end of December 2006 because of the failure of the State governments to submit utilisation certificates under the "Fiscal Responsibility and Budget Management Act of 2004." Time is money it should be remembered at the every level of governance to address the problem truly.

CONSENSUS ORIENTED

There are several actors and as many view points in a given society. Good governance requires mediation of the different interests in society to reach a broad consensus in society on what is in the best interest of the whole community and how this can be achieved. It also requires a broad and long-term perspective on what is needed for sustainable human development and how to achieve the goals of such development. This can only result from an understanding of the historical, cultural and social contexts of a given society or community. Every Naxal-affected State should form an intellectual committee to study and analyze the genesis, socio-economic background and strategies to sort out the problem of Naxalism in that state. And then draft a space and time specific policy how to tackle the issue keeping its specific structure and nature in the state. Eradicating Naxalism, however, is more than a local policing problem. One difficulty has been that, under India's constitution, security is a subject of state governments rather than the centre. So national policy to deal with the Naxalism has been in consistent. In 2004, the government of Andhra Pradesh held abortive peace talks with local Naxalites, while other states continued to fight them.Thus there must be coordination between the center and state government while tackling the Naxal isue.

EQUITY AND INCLUSIVENESS

A society's well being depends on ensuring that all its members feel that they have a stake in it and do not feel excluded from the mainstream of society. This requires all groups, but particularly the most vulnerable, have opportunities to improve or maintain their well being. The ACHR in March 2006 opined that the formation of a separate Ministry for the development of naxalite-affected areas should be considered as a way to bridge the gap between promises and performance. This suggestion has not been taken up seriously by any section of the government, but the political leadership, as well as the bureaucracy, has not been found wanting in setting up a number of government bodies and committees with the ostensible objective of addressing the situation in naxalite-affected regions. Equality and welfare of all is the vision of our constitution. Its inability to transfer its vision in real is the case of Naxalism-growth on the Indian soil. Thus it is important to make the arrangement of equal and non-discriminative atmosphere for all the depressed and oppressed class in political, economic and social system.

EFFECTIVENESS AND EFFICIENCY

Good governance means that processes and institutions produce results that meet the needs of society while making the best use of resources at their disposal. The concept of efficiency in the context of good governance also covers the sustainable use of natural resources and the protection of the environment. The tribal and rural social structures of India are very rich in natural resources as well indigenous knowledge. It would be better to make them capable for generation resources and self employments by providing them proper education and training at their own place.

ACCOUNTABILITY

Accountability is a key requirement of good governance. It involves a relationship between the citizens and the government, which is strengthened by frequent interactions and communications between them. Not only governmental institutions but also the private sector and civil society organizations must be accountable to the public and to their institutional stakeholders. Who is accountable to who varies depending on whether decisions or actions taken are internal or external to an organization or institution. In general an organization or an institution is accountable to those who will be affected by its decisions or actions. Accountability cannot be enforced without transparency and the rule of law. Due to instable government in modern times it is hard to expect their accountability towards the public. But with the ban on criminalization of politics and creation of mass awareness accountability can be ensured.

The words 'governance of the country' appears only in Article 37 of the Constitution in Part IV in the Directive Principles of State Policy but good governance is writ large and implicit in several provision of the Constitution. Time has come to declare right to good governance as a fundamental right under Article 14, 19 and 21 of the Constitution. Indeed Indian constitution adopts the broad concept of a welfare state is generally sensitive to all angles of public life. Hence public wellbeing is the ultimate object of a welfare state.

CONCLUSION

The above discussion evidently shows that Naxalism has acquired a worst form of challenge for governance. Both preventive and curative measures should be adopted for uprooting and curbing Naxalism, so that good governance is possible. Only public-oriented and action-oriented government can contribute substantively in this field. Hence, the strategy will have to be dual: to implement programs and policies that address the pressing needs and demands of the deprived people, especially the scheduled tribes and scheduled castes; and, at the same time, to ensure effective policing and maintenance of law and order. The speedy implementation of land reforms, the redistribution of land, the assurance of tribal rights to forest produce, implementation of development projects and spread of mass education and health facilities are all important steps that must be taken. In fact, it is important not just for the nine States officially categorised as "Naxalite affected," but also for others facing socio-economic unrest to take serious steps to meet basic needs, invest substantial resources in socio-economic development, and, towards this objective, decentralise governance and empower local bodies. If they succeed, there will be greatly reduced space for naxalism and other forms of extremism to grow. In short, Naxalism is the result of non-responsive and non caring attitude of government and the public both so it is their common job to be active, positive and assertive for its removal completely.

REFERENCES

1. *The Economist*, August 17, 2006
2. *Yojna*, February, 2007.
3. Prakash Singh, IPS, *The Naxalite Movement in India*, Press Club.
4. K. Satyanarayan, IPS, *Know Your Enemy*.
5. Vijay Shankar Chaturvedi, *Naxali Aatank Aur Sonabhadra*, Press Club, Sonabhadra.
6. Andrew Heywood, *Politics Foundations*, New York, 1997.
7. www.hindustantimes.com
8. www.ipcs.org
9. www.satp.org
10. S.D. Muni, *Maoist Insurgency in Nepal*, ORF, Rupa Publications, New Delhi, 2003.
11. Frontline, Vol. 24, September, 2007.
12. www.india-seminar.com
13. The Hindu, September 21, 2005.
14. www.undp.org.
15. www.naxalwatch.com
16. www.unescp.org

4

ETHNICITY AND REGIONALISM IN NORTH-EAST INDIA *SOME RECENT TRENDS*

Dr. Ashutosh Pandey

INTRODUCTION

"On the social plane, we have in India a society based on the principle of graded inequality which means elevation for some and degradation for others, on the economic plane, we have some who have immense wealth as against many who live in abject poverty. On the 20th January 1950, we are going to enter into a life of contradictions. In Politics we will have equality and in social and economic life we will have inequality. We must remove this contradiction at the earliest possible moment or else, those who suffer from inequality will blow up the structure of political democracy which this assembly has so laboriously built up."

B.R. Ambedkar, moving the find reading of the Constitution in the Constituent Assembly of India, November 29, 1949.

India's North-East is a region at the edge of the Indian subcontinent, sandwiched between Bhutan China, Myanmar and Bangladesh, more then 220 ethnic groups live here, all of them with an age-old history, their own culture, custom, religion and language. Since the end of British Colonial rule in 1947 the multi-faced North-East was made to merge with the union of India. And over the years seven states were formed, Assam, Meghalaya, Tripura, Mizoram, Arunachal, Pradesh, Nagaland, and Manipur, many refer to them as "seven sisters". Political movements for autonomy or separate nationhood of certain ethnic groups have been quite frequent in the eastern region of India. No other movement in independent India has proved so intractable. Even after vivisection of the region into seven units, most of which are of the size of a district in other status, there is no complete peace.[1] Ethnic assertion in more quantitative terms refers to an increase in ethnic killings and losses of property-both private and public. It Ted Gurr is to be believed, during the period 1945-1989 more than 200 groups "openly resisted the terms of their incorporation in status, controlled by other groups. Their grievance about discrimination and threats to group's identity . . . motivated hundreds of protest movements."[2] One wonders whether Gurr has taken the north-eastern India into his accounts, the number could surely be higher than what his estimate says. Indeed, there is reason to think that ethnic killings since 1971 have acquired a mass and anomic character.[3] all that continues in face of various concessions granted to meet ant the regional and sub-regional aspirations. Separate statehood with local autonomy has been granted to allay the fear of dominance by larger communities. While the situation has been saved to some extent from reaching a breaking point, the end of hostilities and restoration of normalcy is still far off. Obviously, the differentiated identities have come to develop to a point where emergence of a new corporate or federated identity may take its own time provided things are not allowed to drift to a point of no return.

Regionalism is a much used as well as abused term in contemporary Indian political vocabulary. In their zeal for national unity and integration, scholars have usually over played the disruptive consequences of regionalism while underplaying its constrictive implications. In the early sixties a foreign of server speculated that India faced the damager us alternatives of either balkanization for regional autonomy gained ground.[4] One scholar goes to the extent of saying that "what appears, certain is that, whether overtly or covertly, the 'ism' that rules India today is regionalism."[5]

According to Iqbal Narain, regionalism in the context of India is a vague concept and has both positive and negative dimensions. Positively, it embodies a guest for fulfillment on the part of and area. In this perspective, it constitutes a true expression of federation and not to be considered as alibi for the balkanization of the country. Negatively, regionalism "reflects a psyche of relative deprivation resulting from specific grievances".[6]

The reversal of this trend resulting in the emergence of the differentiated identities, therefore, merit a serious attention into the questions when, why and show it occurred?

PRIMORDIAL AND LOCALISM

The use of primordial ties in organizing movement can be understood within the context of competitive politics, modernization, inter-State migration and Government politics. Under the impact of competitive politics, caste, tribe and other social categories have become politicized. In other words, movement leaders tend to look upon the social categories as natural political units.[7] The forces of modernization enhance people's aspirations and expectations and intensity competition for employment, housing and other welfare values. Challenges may arise from multiple sources, such as government policies, economics competition, etc. On several occasions movements were organized on the basis of primordial loyalties when economic threats were perceived by movement participants.

In recent times movement participants tend to identity themselves by the place they be long, call themselves Bhumiputras (sons of the soil), and distinguish themselves from the non-locals who are often migrants.[8] Inter-state migration leady to movements in those regions where an ethnic division of labor eructs. Those who express disgust at the phenomena of primordial and localism misread the social basis of India's political life. There is nothing sinister about the use of primordial and other attachments in politics so long as that does not incite violence and destroy civil peace. The point is succinctly put through by Clifford Geerts who observes that:

> "In modern societies the lifting of such primordial ties to the level of political supremacy through it has more and more come to be deplored as pathological. To an increasing degree national unity is maintained not by calls to blood and land, but by vague, intermittent and routine allegiance to a civil state (civil ties) supplemented to a greater or lesser extent by governmental use of power."[9]

ETHNIC GROUP FORMATION IN THE NORTH-EAST

In a very broad way the north-eastern region can be divided into two parts: (i) the narrow strips of plains known as Brahmaputra or Assam Valley—the total area being 56, 274 sq. km.; (ii) The hilly and plateau region consisting of Himalayan high peaks in the north and Meghalaya plateau the south and forming a girdle around the Brahmaputra Valley. The latter region however is not a very compact and homogenous one. Thus each small area witnesses flourishing of its own distinct and autonomous culture.

SEPARATE STATEHOOD

Yet again the problem of Naxalism has assumed alarming proportions especially with the latest happenings in Orissa, Andhra Pradesh and Karnataka.This movement was originally carried out by the landless against the landlord. However, at present many vested interests guide it. There is also the fear of having a corridor extending from UP-Nepal border passing through Jharkand, Chattisgarh and reaching up to Andhra Pradesh. Naxals also have strong presence in some parts of Maharashtra (Gadchiroli and Chandrapur districts), Orissa and Karnataka. They have their presence in 15 States and 160 districts. In some districts of Andhra, there is total collapse of the governmental machinery.

Naxals have a different *modus operandi* than other enemies of the state. The are driven by a strong ideology and command local support to a great degree. These two factors make it extremely difficult for the security forces to tackle them. The 'low intensity' conflict has various facets to it and has to be carried out at the different levels simultaneously. During the short stay in Naxal-infested Gadchiroli district of Maharashtra the author was fortunate to gain a first hand idea of this low intensity conflict. It is just impossible to locate naxalites, they mingle with the local populace and enjoy considerable support from them. A police team cannot do anything without definitive intelligence inputs-which are hard to come by. Police at times are not able to match the weaponry of the Naxalites and this in turn affects their moral.

To tackle the problem of naxalities it is imperative that the government outsmarts them in their own game. Use of force is not the only solution, it may pacify the situation for a while but not in long term. Naxalism has ideological roots, they draw their thought from Maoism. (Naxalities are also called Maoists). Added to this they are local heroes - created by either goodwill or gun. This has added to the difficulty for the government.

Naxalism has to be fought at various fronts - security, ideological, social and economic. The civic administration and the security establishment have to co-ordinate the strategies. Local population has to be taken into confidence and self-help groups should be formed–Andhra Pradesh has benefited greatly from this. It is essential to counter the ideology of Naxalism with the ideology of the government. Here the role of senior officers is crucial.

The administration has failed in delivering good governance in the naxal-infested areas, especially the remote villages. Reaching out to people, helping them and most importantly empowering them will be needed for a lasting solution. Finally, the security forces have to be given a clear plan of action and full support by the government- both state and center. The lessons from the failed peace talks have to be kept in mind in future course of action.

The demand for a separate state is not wholly a recent phenomenon. Before independence come to India in 1947 a demand for a Sikh homeland was made by some Sikh leaders. After independence a few now States emerged in the north-east (Nagaland in 1963 and Mizoram in 1987) as a consequence of separatist movements. The Bodo tribes demand a separate State on the north bank of river. In Manipur the Revolutionary People's Front (RPF) urged the Prime Minister of India to "acknowledge that Manipur was an independent country and never a part they want to live happily and peacefully which calls for the right to, 'live freely'.[10]

India's experience shows that antipathy between the local population and the migrants may occasion separatist movement. Article 19 of the Constitution of India specifies that all citizens "shall have the right to move freely throughout the territory of India" and "to reside and settle in any part of the territory of India."

From the review of the early friends during the British rule, however, it is evident that the concern for one's own identity did not make the people of the north-east isolationist and oblivious of or indifferent to the emerging 'great nationalism' or the larger Indian identity.

Segregationist feedings did not develop even when objective conditions favored such a growth. The growth of ideologies differed in intensity and also in terms of emergence of supportive structure. It is also obvious that the quest for wider fraternities was more among the emerging modern elite than among the traditional chiefs.

INTER-ELITE CONFLICT AND PROBLEM OF REGIONALISM

Similarly, the articulation of issues of language, religion and ethnicity and the differences on these counts appear to be only a manifestation of the problem at different levels. Thus a deeper probe brings out that the issues of language, etc. and other primordial factors came to be articulated only in the wake of emerging conflicts between the political elites at various levels because of clash of interests and consequent distrust of one another, besides the political factors straining the relationship between various leaders, there were important economic factors which contributed to conflicts among various sets of elite at different levels. Among them two major factors may be identified here for their singular role: first, issue of land reform and, record, problems concerning job opportunities in civil service and their modern occupations. The issue of land ownership and land reform has been the most contentions in the hill areas and lately in the plains also.

Against the general impression of tribal societies being more egalitarian, the fact is that the khasis, the mizos and some other communities have had some form of feudal or land-lord system. When politics operates in that way, the elites tend to generalize their conflicts and valid up movements.

CONCLUSION

To say this all is not to deny the role of socio-economic backwardness and the fear of exploitation by outsiders in such movements. They do play a vital role and in the case of the north-east they have played even a greater role when compared to other areas. An analysis of the past political developments may have only an academic or historical value, but in the case of north-east region that is not so. The hopes that the north-east will be quiet and stable after grant of autonomy to the stirred communities have not materialized. Almost all the political turmoil and consequently disruption of normal political processes. But even a trend of greater significance is that some sort of supra-regional movement is in the offing as the rebel groups are working out under standing and alliances among themselves. In the long run, this may unity certain kinds of political forces but in a different way and for a different cause. The orientation of them is culturally anti-centre, it not anti-national. Given greater skill, attention and accommodative spirit, the centre can handle the problem more conveniently today than tomorrow. Two remarks by way of conclusion. First, through every movement tend to unsettle the social and political arrangements they are not malignant growths. They convey the message that all is not well with the system of governing. Second, movements suggest that all people are not disposed to tolerate unhappiness with and negligence by the incumbent authorities.

The dichotomy between the elites and the masses, the economic chasm between the affluent and the deprived, and the gap between the 'have' and 'have-not' regions are continuing issues of concern for India's nation building endeavor. The goals of unity democracy, development, justice and autonomy can be achieved in the long run 'only through participant and accommodative models of politics.' A democratic, socialist, secular and federal framework is ideally suited to achieve these goals. "But", as kothari aptly observes, "It is necessary that those in command of frame work-the class-act with commitment to the people and to the binding nexus that can hold them gather. This is the test of the present and the emerging generations of the Indian leadership. In the final analysis it is also the test of the Indian people."[11]

NOTES AND REFERENCES

1. But this is also apparent, as Rajni Kothari sums up the Implications, 'Politics in India have served to Provide a 'model' for the Integration of the Various Diversities and Cleavages into a Common Framework, Led to an interplay between parochial demands and systemic Outputs, and Through such an Interplay Challenged the Established System of Institutions and Symbols Towards New Thresholds of Performance. Rajni Kothari, Politics in India, New Delhi, orient Longmans, 1971, p. 356.

2. Ted Gurr, Robert, *Minorities At Risk*, Washing to D.C. US Institute of Peace Press, 1992, p. 92.

3. Das, Samir Kumar, *Bichchinnatar Katha: Uttar Purbo Bharat Barsha* (in Bengali), *Nandan*, March 1996. pp. 41-6.

4. See Harrison, Selig S., *India: The Most Dangerous Decades*, USA: Princeton, 1960.

5. Roy, A.K. "Almost Extinct Indian", *The Statesman*, Calcutta, March 11, 1986, p. 8.
6. Narain, Iqbal, "Cultural Pluralism, National Integration and Democracy in India," in K.R. Bomball (ed.), *National Power and State Autonomy,* Meerut: Meenakshi Prakashan, 1978, p. 186.
7. Regarding the politicization of caste Kothari wrote, "By Drawing the Caste System into Its Web of Organization, Politics finds Materials for its Articulation and Moulds it into its Own Design. In making Politics their Sphere of Activity, Caste and Kin Groups on the Other Hand get a Chance to Assert Their Identity and to Strive for Positions . . . Politicians Mobilize Caste Groupings and Identities in Organizing their Power. They find in it and Extremely well Articulated and Flexible Basis for Organizations, something that may have been Structured in Terms of Status Hierchy, but something that is also Available for Political Manipulation . . . Kothari, Rajni, (ed.) *Caste in Indian Politics*, New Delhi : Orient Longman Limited, 1970, p. 5.
8. The Constitution of India Recognizes the Right to Migrate.
9. Cliffored Geertz Quoted by M. Ross Barnet, *The Politics of Cultural Nationalism in South India*. Princeton University Press, 1976.
10. *The Telegraph*, 2 June, 1997, p. 6.
11. Kothari, Rajni, op. cit., "Nation Building and Political Development" in S.C. Dube (ed.), *India Since Independence*, New Delhi: Vikas, 1977, pp. 530-531.

5

GOOD GOVERNANCE
WAY TO SOLVE INTERNAL CONFLICTS

Dr. Deepak Kumar Pandey

Power differentials in society assure that some groups will exploit others and constitute a built-in source of tension and conflict in social systems. Although conflict is an inevitable feature of all societies, but it may be more common within communities, that encompass diverse socio-cultural identities and economic disparities. Paul Bohannan opined that, "society is impossible without conflict. But society is worse than impossible without control of conflict."[1] The costs of violent conflict are often disproportionately high compared to the original stakes, and they are often borne by people who have little control over decision-making or influence over those who can reduce violence.

With the occurrence of continuous violent attacks in different parts of country, with ever changing targets, there is obvious question in the mind of common man that how far we are safe as denizen of nation? Security environment inside the territorial boundary of nation is continuously deteriorating and State seems to be helpless in stemming the tide. People look up to state structures for protection and feel betrayed when they lost their near and dear ones in extremist violence.

Since conflicts are often brought on by processes implicit in the internal structures of one or both of the contending parties, a change of these structures might end such conflicts and also their recurrence. Johan Galtung owes the origin of conflict in the maladjustments of structure which creates tension and inequity of any kind. Inequality hinders the smooth progress of society. It undermines the individual potentiality and cause frustration and conflict in society, which Galtung termed as structural violence. According to Johan Galtung, structural violence is a system of differential, unequal access to the means for closing the gap between the actual and the potential, where those at 'the bottom' of some hierarchically structured rational system.[2] Radical transformation of competing parties has often been advocated as a way to solve the conflicts. But this radical transformation must not be very quick to disturb society's equilibrium. Less sweeping changes in the domestic social systems and politics of states might be both safer and more effective, if such changes get carried over unmittingly. These changes should be in the direction of increasing capabilities and potentialities of common man to use the available resources in best possible way, increasing their stake in system and thus lowering the chance of conflict and strife.

Here, question is not the sincerity of state to tackle the extremism, but the way of approaching towards extremism to neutralize it matters more. This extremism is offshoot of far greater problem entrenched in the society. Before applying any approach, we have to go into the generic causes of conflict; otherwise it will come out again and again in the favourable environ. In most of the cases of internal conflict, reason lies in the inequity and denial of those basic human needs which are essential for the dignified life. The replacement of the existing culture of violence by a culture of peace, human rights and democracy can only be achieved in a longer perspective.

Experience shows that, although political and economic changes may be rapid, cultural changes, in particular changes in the behavioural patterns of individuals, groups and nations take time.[3] In fact, conflict in all true sense is about change in social structure and institutions, in the distribution of resources at many levels. Conflict by its very nature is governed by two sets of issues. What changes shall occur and at whose expense? This expense should be minimized for maintaining equilibrium of the system. John Burton puts it as, "it is the means to change, the means by which our social values of welfare, security, justice and opportunities for personal development can be achieved."[4]

This replacement of culture demands the good governance from the state structures. Pattern of governance, that enshrines with democratic norms, free from corruption and biasness with a deep sense of sympathy towards the have nots. This pattern of governance needs a higher degree of motivation to work selflessly for the sake of nation building. Upto 90% of strife and conflict can be neutralize by rectifying the pattern of governance and administrative attitude. With quick and transparent judicial and administrative system, conflict can be prevented to be erupted out.

Conflict situation is normally said to arise between parties, who perceive that they possess mutually incompatible objectives. But in most of internal conflicts in larger pretext, objectives of state and contending parties are not incompatible and here lies the solution. This positivity can only be nurtured through good governance; governance which entails democracy. Because resolution of conflicts leads to new set of relationships. Democracy has the highest acceptance in any matrix of governance in any structure. Democracy in itself embodies the notion of liberty, identity and stake of shareholders. So, governance by democratic means also entails the stake of people involved in it fulfilling their identity needs. Conflict resolution in a more dynamic form requires not only the attitudinal change but to conflict resolution complete democratic transformation and respect for human rights is sine-qua-non.

National security perspective on conflict classifies conflicts by the threats they are thought to pose to the security of the state. The failure of normal constitutional and legal system abrupt the internal structure of society. Internal conflict is defined as the existence of organized groups within state which enjoy some degree of intra-group legitimacy and coherence and whose demands and interests have not been readily reconciled or resolved within existing domestic institutional (political, judicial or economic) mechanisms. This suggests that internal conflict within a state is linked to the inability of existing institutional mechanisms at the national or local level to adequately manage or address the concerns of disaffected groups, resulting in the resort to violence.[5]

Competition and disagreement between groups are usually found in all political system. In the Indian context where politics or representative system which is functioning at the moment has utterly failed and is not upto the mark in prevention of disputes and conflicts. The idea of representation as publicly accountable action on behalf of the electorate has collapsed into a vicious politics of interests based on region, caste and religion, in which identities and claims are beyond discussion or evaluation. Electoral politics has become rank opportunism. National and other identity groups typically define their actions as consistent with their own interpretation of legal conventions. They will accept laws of the land only when they feel that this land is also theirs, they have their stake in prevailing institutions and they have shelter to save them and space to stand over. Their fight is for proper space in all spheres and their basic rights of dignified life. Difference and inequality aggravates the psychological factor inside the individual to move towards conflict. Precarious living conditions, poverty, displacement and human suffering create their own vicious cycle often associated with communal violence that may further entangle communities in the dynamics of the conflict.[6]

While problems such as human rights violations, displacement and poverty may themselves arise due to conflict, they may also contribute to a further escalation of violence. The implications for the affected communities are inevitably multifaceted.[7] John Burton has hypothesized a link between frustration and basic needs for identity, security, autonomy, dignity and bending. He attempts to correlate psychology with other tangible and intangible gains as cause of conflicts.[8] 'Revolutionary' violence that persists for decades, as has Left extremism in India, must be evaluated by criteria other than the general 'causal' approach that seeks to justify it in terms of historical wrongs and contemporary inequalities, or the presumption of its intrinsic beneficence. As one commentator observes, "Since this movement has had a controversial and turbulent existence on India's political stage for close to six decades, its leaders must attempt a socio-political audit of their efforts - from the point of view of their own objectives and its impact on the people they are fighting for."[9]

Menace of extremism flourish in the favourable environ of inequality and discrimination prevalent in the society, where some section of citizenry has been denied their basic human needs by influential section of society. This extremism should be neutralize by state structure in all possible way, where approach should be broad and positive. And this positivity is best spread by providing good quality education to all. Hashim Queraishi, once a terrorist who hijacked a plane in 1971, which was first hijacking of Asia, transformed himself into a reformist with the help of education. He is now president of JKDLF (Jammu Kashmir Democratic Liberation Front) and also contests elections in Kashmir. He now believes in democratic process and peace.[10] When a terrorist can be accommodated and transformed through self education, why these some section of betrayed people cannot be accommodated in the institutional mechanism with some initiative?

The need of the hour is right approach. Approach which creates trust in the minds of people that state structure is with them, it should be seems that structures are there to redress their grievances not to aggravate them. And this onus will be upon government structure along with NGOs to provide good governance. Negative approach of mere policing may aggravate the problem to dangerous level. Policing should be there to check the availability of arms, to control the notorious elements, and strict vigilance should be made on the external inputs, which activate the extremism, with strong intelligence network. Policing should not be of suppressive nature, based on colonial model. Molestation of common people by security personnel may lead to alienation towards state. If they do not feel secure by the personals that are responsible for the safety of citizenry of state, why they feel themselves as part of citizenry? So, a sympathetic approach of police may help in healing their wounds. The irony is that the state response to Naxalism remains incoherent and directionless. *The Central Coordination Committee* (CCC) of Naxalite affected States headed by the Union Home Ministry has met at least fifteen times since its inception to discuss the problem, but has not been able to evolve any comprehensive strategy to tackle the threat. Shri Ajit Jogi, ex chief minister of Chhatisgarh opined that, the naxalite problem cannot be dealt with as a purely military one. "It has to be tackled at the socio-economic and political levels. One has to understand the root causes why naxalism gained ground in the State and try to remove those causes."[11]

Naxal extremism and other internal conflicts gain strength from people's grievances and their support. Alienated section attaches them with naxal extremist ideology. So a quick and transparent grievance redressal mechanism is necessary to curb the extremist feeling at primary level. If naxal ideology takes strength from people's dissatisfaction, why government structures may not solve the problem by attaching themselves with people having efficient, prompt and quick delivery system at the receiving end? To break the nexus governance pattern should make efforts to attach with the common people with sympathy. If government institutions have to win, they have to attack on the strength of extremism, not on the common poor people. If alienated and dejected section relates to government institutions and policies, half battle is won. But, the corrupt practices in the implementation of policies may make situation worse. There is no need to frame the plethora of policies and plans, existing plans are enough to solve the problems. But problem lies in the proper implementation and pattern of governance. If Public distribution system is not working well (as in most of the cases) and unable to feed starving bellies, BPL cards are not available to entitled people, safe drinking water is not available, proper health facilities are not there in place to take care of poor fellows, mediators and contractors are engulfing the funds of different schemes, how can one expect that the poor common man will be faithful to government institutions? How system will prevent them to follow the extremist path? How the poor children, who don't have access to good quality education and food, be prevented from being aggressive?

The Asian Centre for Human Rights (ACHR) reflects a similar opinion. A note on naxal conflict prepared by ACHR in July 2007, pointed out that, "there has been no dearth of development schemes in India, but the implementation of such schemes perennially remained problematic and implementation of the schemes in naxalite affected areas almost came to virtual halt because of the increased conflict. An estimated Rs 6,500 crores meant for implementation of the *National Rural Employment Guarantee Programme* were not spent during 2005-2006 and Rs 1,522.90 crores for development of tribals could not be released by the Ministry of Tribal Affairs to various state governments by the end of December 2006 because of the failure of the state governments to submit utilization certificates under the Fiscal Responsibility and Budget Management Act of 2004."[12] The *Centre for Environment and Food Security* (CEFS), a Delhi- based organization that had conducted a survey of 100 villages to assess the implementation of NREGS, said that it was not the epidemic of cholera but the cancer of corruption that was killing hundreds of poor tribal people and crippling millions of them.[13]

Naxal extremism cannot be neutralize by propagating and supporting violence from another group as seen in the case of Salwa Judum of Chhattisgarh. Salwa Judum which means peace mission in Gondi language is not infact a peace mission. It leads to anarchy and complete failure of system, because onus to protect its citizen is upon government, not upon some section of violent militant groups with their inherent interests. As for the government, which has been all along claiming that Salwa Judum is a self- initiated people's movement against Maoist oppression and that it is only providing logistical support to "people suffering at the hands of naxalites", should not be an excuse to shy away from their responsibilities. People support is necessary for government structure to fight against naxal extremism, but this support should not b violent.

Many scholars estimated that millions of poor people are displaced since independence and only about 30% of them have been properly rehabilitated and resettled. In case of tribal people, this estimate is as low as 20%. Thus a huge section of poor native people are displaced and are without shelter and job. Not only this, but nowadays displacement and landlessness because of SEZs have become a cause of concern, because it aggravate the inequality and increase the divide between haves and have-nots. State structure, capturing the fertile land of poor people in the name development and industrial growth, and not making the people part of that developmental process bounds them to be aggressive and violent. It should not be that development and industrial growth not be made, but in the process of that development, people should be part of that. For the development to be sustainable and not as cause for conflict, it should be people friendly, not to the mere advantage of capitalist section. Land reform all over the nation has been necessitated in the wake of new situation. Land for each part should be clearly marked, for agricultural purpose, for ecological equilibrium and also for industrial growth.

Here in this process democratic governance through means of Panchayat may play an effective role. PESA (*Panchayat Act Extension to Schedule Areas*) Act, 1996, that gives tribal Panchayats a fair degree of control over their land

and requires that all activity involving minor minerals and development projects have the expressed consent of Panchayat. This Act should not be confined only to minor minerals and development projects but to all the development projects. And this provision of PESA Act 1996 should be incorporated in the Panchayat Act, that would be applicable all over the country.

Pattern of development is also related with pattern of governance. Good governance, which demands the sensitivity of institutions, structures or delivery system towards the demands and aspirations of common people. Improving human security requires sustained economic growth and human development with the improvement in governance. Weak delivery system, which hinders the delivey of goods like health, education, drinking water, sanitation, infrastructure are directly linked to the pattern of governance. Hospitals without medicines and doctors, schools and colleges without teachers, police structure with colonial mindset, corrupt bureaucratic structure, water with pollutants, bellies without food and hands without job does not ensure the security of common individuals. The pursuit of human security means that institutions must function as change and development agents, which alter the status quo position. In the process of governance when internal conflicts or contradictions, emerge or sharpen between the different sections of a class or between different ruling classes within the alliance they are sought to be managed through bargaining, conflicts and compromises.[14] The then UN Secretary-General Kofi Annan has asserted that "good governance at the local, national and international levels is perhaps the single most important factor in promoting development and advancing the cause of peace"[15]

The rank and file of this naxalites army are not hard nosed ideologues, but people who are totally disillusioned with the current system of governance. Their major concerns are not about the creation of a classless society but issues like; land for the tiller, education, fair market practices, right to forest produce, responsive governance and a host of such basic issues. If this assertion is true then what holds them together?

Anger! Anger that seethes through the very being of human existence against inequity imposed due to sheer apathy about the conditions in which such vast numbers of humanity are condemned to live and die.Democratization, participation in decision-making, accountability of decision-makers, respect for the rule of law and human rights, inclusive, equitable and fair rules and institutions are key governance issues which are closely linked to the empowerment of people and communities. Without effective governance, people could not be empowered. And unless people and communities are empowered to let their voices to be heard or to participate in decision-making, governance is not feasible.[16] Cake should be enlarged to be shared by every stakeholder. In order to achieve the goal of human security, sustainable development has been considered essential, and for the sustainable development, sensitive governance structures are sine qua non.

REFERENCES

1. Paul Bohannan (ed.), *Law and Warfare: Studies in the Anthropology of Conflict*, Natural History Press, Garden City, New York, 1967, Preface, p. xii.
2. Johan Galtung 'Peace, Violence and Peace Research', *Journal of Peace Research*, 6, 1969, p. 171.
3. SIPRI-UNESCO Handbook on "Peace, Security and Conflict Prevention".
4. John Burton World Society, Cambridge University Press, Cambridge and New York, 1972, pp. 137-138.
5. "Internal Conflict and Regional Security in South Asia Approaches, Perspectives and Policies", *UNIDIR*, Geneva 2003, p. 8.
6. Albert Bandura, *Aggression: A Social Learning Analysis*, Prentice-Hall, Engle-Wood Cliffs, New Jersey, 1973. p. 9.
7. *Ibid*, p. 11.
8. J.W. Burton, *Conflict: Resolution and Prevention*, Macmillan, Landon and St. Martin's Press, New York, 1990 a, pp. 33-34
9. Ajay K. Mehra, "Failing Revolution", The Pioneer, March 10, 2000.
10. Based on programme Salaam Jindagi Broadcasted on *NDTV INDIA* news channel on 03/08/08 from 6.30 to 7.00 pm.

11. Purnima S. Tripathi, "Strategy gone Awry", *Frontline*, Sep. 21, 2007, p. 17.
12. Venkitesh Ramakrishnan, "Naxal terror", *Frontline*, Sep 21, 2007, p. 8
13. Prafulla Das, "Deathly inaction", *Frontline*, Sep. 21, 2007, p. 39.
14. Javed Alam, "Class, Political and National Dimensions of The State Autonomy Movements in India", in Akhtar Majeed (ed.), Regionalism Developmental Tensions in India, Cosmo Publications, New Delhi, 1984, p. 45.
15. United Nations, General Assembly 2002, p. 11.
16. Human Security Now, *Commission on Human Security*, New York, 2003, p. 68.

6

NAXALITE MOVEMENT IN ORISSA

Dr. Jayant Kumar Parida

The Naxalite Movement has been a significant socio-political movement of our times. As a movement it takes its name from a peasant uprising, which occurred in May 1967 at Naxalbari in the State of West Bengal. It was started under the leadership of Charu Majumdar and Kanu Sanyal, who defined the objective of the movement as 'seizure of power through revolution'. After its four decades of existence it has emerged as a decisive force in the country. At present the movement has spread over 170 districts in 15 States of India (Mohanty: 2006). Naxal influence has been spread to nearly 40 per cent of the country's geographical area, with affected population going up to 35 per cent (*The Hindu*: 2006). Rise of Naxal activities in such a mass scale has forced Prime Minister of India to describe it as "single biggest internal challenge" (Singh: 2007). Of the total 12,476 police stations in the country, Naxal activities have been reported in 460 police stations (Yojana: 2007).In their strong holds in about 55 districts in 12 states they run parallel government (Mehera: 2007).

In our country the Naxalite activities are found in backward areas in different states in north and West India and concentrated in a slender passage way running from Bihar in north-east, through Jharakhand and Chhattisgarh in the centre, down to Orissa and Andhra Pradesh in the South. It is this 'Red Corridor' that has become the operational field of the Naxalities (Banarjee: 2006). During the past few decades, Naxal activities gained a mass base among peasants, adivasis, dalits and labouring classes. Particularly, Naxal activities have reported in hilly, forest and backward areas of the country which are traditionally remained beyond the reach of any development projects, social welfare schemes and agencies of administration (Gupta: 2006).

ORIGIN OF NAXALITE MOVEMENT IN INDIA

The Naxalite movement owes its origins to the turbulent days of 1960-70 period when communist revolutions broke away from the parent Communist Party of India (Marxist) CPI (M) and along with others founded the Communist Party of India-Marxist Leninst (CPI-L). More than 30 years after the adaptation of CPI (ML) programmes, its other follower groups like *People's War Group* (PWG) activities in Andhra Pradesh, the *Maoist Communist Centre* (MCC) merged together and formed Communist Party of India-Maoist (CPI-Maoist). After their merger, they are trying to woo their splinter groups and have also consolidated their frontal organizations into "Revolutionary Democratic Front (RDF) and 'People's Democratic Front of India (PDFI) to intensify their mass contract programme.

The route of movement that has mapped in 1967 at the time of Naxalbari uprising still remains the same. Ideologically, the movement accepts Marxism-Leninism-Maoism as its ideology and is committed to completing a 'new democratic revolution' in India before passing on to achieve its socialist goals. The Naxalites believe that revolution to be carried out and completed through an armed struggle for seizure of power. The Naxalite revolution is directed against imperialism, feudalism and 'comprador bureaucratic capitalism'. The movement also supports the fight against social oppression particularly, untouchablility and casteism (Gupta: 2006).

NAXALITE MOVEMENT IN ORISSA

Though Naxalites activities have gained momentum in recent times, as a movement it is quite old in Orissa. For a log time Orissa's tryst with Naxalite movement was reduced as a split over effect from the neighboring state Andhra Pradesh. However, Orissa has a long history of Communist and peasant movements. The Naxalite movement in Orissa emerged in the early 1960s as a peasant movement and tribal movement on the issue of 'land to tillers' by Communist party of India in Ganjam and Koraput district (Down to Earth: 2001). Subsequently the movement spread to tribal pockets in other districts, resulting in protest against discrimination in access to non-timber forest produce and alienation of tribal land. Later on the movement spread quickly to other disadvantaged class, landless people and intellectuals.

However, during the Past few years, extremists have gained a mass base and strengthened their position in the backward and less developed areas of Orissa. More particularly, Naxal activities have found in South, South-West and Western hilly, and forest areas of the state where there is lack of employment opportunities, low level of literacy, high share of Scheduled Castes and Scheduled Tribes population, high mortality, high share of agricultural labourer, low per capita food gain production, low level of road length and low per capita income. According to latest report, Naxals have intensity their activities in 15 districts (half of the territories) of the State. These affected districts are: Koraput, Malkanagiri, Nabarangapur, Rayagada, Gajapati, Sudergarh, Keonjhar, Sambalpur, Kandhamal, Deogarh, Jharasuguda, Jajpur, Mayurbhanja, and Nayagarh. Besides the above mentioned districts, more recently, Maoist activities are reported from pockts of Boudh, Dhenkanal and Angul districts of Orissa. The 'Red Corridor' from Saranda forest in Jharakhand in one hand to Rairkhol forest in Sambalpur are the other hand is now chief centre of Maoist activities in orissa (Kajur: 2007)

Among the extremist groups Maoist Centre (MCC) and *Peoples War Group* (PWG) are activities in Orissa, MCC outfit is found active in Sundergarh, Keonjahar, Sambalpur, Mayurbhanja, Deogarh, Jajpur, PWG has presence in Malkanagiri, Koraput, Rayagada, Ganjam, Gajqapati and Nabarangapur. Besides the above, CPI-Red Flag and CPI-ML has a minimal influence in Rayagada and Ganjam district. However, aftrer the merger of MCC and PWG, they have formed CPI(Maoist). After the formation of CPI (Maoist), the Naxal Movement has spread to new areas like Kandhamal, Deogarh, Jharasuguda, Jajpur, and Angul(Jha:2003). Presently, there are three zonal committees of CPI(Maosist) functioning in Orissa. These are: (1) Andhra Pradesh-Orissa boarder special Zonal Committee (AOBSZC); (2) Jharakhand-Bihar-Orissa Boarder Special Zonal Committee (ZBOBSZC) and Dandakaranya Special Zonal Committee (DSZC) (Kajpur: 2005). The Naxalite outfits operating in Orissa are in constant touch with their counterparts in the neighbouring States. They procure arms, ammunition from illegal arms market of Bihar, Uttar Pradesh and insurgents groups operating in N.E. States. A significant proportion of their weaponry is a consequence of looting of state armory and police stations. The Naxalite also reported to set up their army manufacturing factories in Dandakaranya. They also get arms from ISI (Telegraph: 2004).

The Naxalite movement has undergone constant mutation since the 1960s. There have been major changes in their strategies, training and fire power. As a result, they are now equipped with better arms, ammunition, weapons and are capable of launching surprise attacks. During the last couple of years, the Naxalities have raised scale of their operations in Orissa. Land mining of Police and CRPF vans and buses, ambushes on large patrols, apart, they have made daring raids on district head quarters town in Koraput on 6th February, 2004 to take away huge quantities of arms and ammunitions. They have attacked Kalimela Police Station in 2001 and Golpadar Police Station in 2003. In the year 2008, extremists have significantly raised their military operations.

On 17th February 2008 they attacked Nayagarah headquarters town and taken away huge quantities of arms and ammunitions and 14 people were killed in the Naxalite attack (Financial: Express, 2008). At Malakanagiri district, the Maoist has blown up police convey and 24 policemen were killed by them. In an another incident, two anti-Naxal force boat of Andhra Pradesh police were drowned by the Naxalities in Balimela on 29th June, 2008 and 50 Policemen were killed in that operation (*Times of India*: 2008). On 23rd August, 2008, the CPI(Maoist) have claimed to have killed the VHP leader Swamy Lakhmanananda Swaraswti at his Jalespata Ashrama in Kandhamal district which has erupted communal violence in Orissa. (*Times of India*: 2008)

What are the possible reasons for the growth of extremist activities in a peace loving state, like Orissa? Of course, no single reason could be attributed for this metaphoric growth of Naxal movement in Orissa. However, the upsurge of Naxalism in Orissa reveals that today's explosive situation is largely due to people's discontentment with system, poor governance, bureaucratic apathy, dominance of land owing communities, cultural discrimination and continuous underdevelopment of the region. Critics are of the opinion that ill thought out of development strategy is the prime reason for the dominance of Naxalities in the South and South Western part of Orissa.

Though a rich state in terms of minerals and natural resources, Orissa has not made any significant progress so far as the development of the state and its people are concerned. The on going process of development has not benefited much to the rural peole, particularly the western and southern belts of Orissa which are called store house of mines and minerals. Orissa continues one of the porest state of the country and about 47 per cent people (80 per cent in tribal areas) still remained below poverty line. Unemployment problem remained rampant in the tribal areas. No doubt several industries and development projects have come up n the areas. But due to ill thought out development strategy many people have been displaced and due to poor resettlement and rehabilitation operations majority of inhabitants of the area ended up with lower incomes, less land then before, less work opportunities, inferior housing, less access to common resources, worse nutrition and physical and mental health. Taking advantage of the poor settlement and rehabilitation operations, acute poverty and socio-economic exploitation, the Maoist outfits have win over the local people as their formidable support base (Kujpur: 2007).

Land alienation issues continue to be the most powerful slogan of the Naxalite movement. Because of this issue Naxalies have been able to consolidate their position in the tribal pockets of Orissa. Manipulation of land records is the single largest problem of the rural tribal poor. The unsatisfactory state of land records contributed a lot to the problem of land alienation. The tribals were never legally recognized as owners of their land, which they have been activating for generations. The second important factors resulting in the problem of land are reduced to the level of share croppers though the land remains to be in their name. Third problem is the 'encroachment' which is diverting the tribals of their land. This is a common problem in the Naxalite infested districts of Orissa where systematic manipulation is being done with the date of settlement of land disputes, ante-dating etc. to be claim tribal lands.

Another reason for the rise of extremist activities is lack of 'Naxal Policy'. Though Naxalism remained as a major socio-economic and political problem for the state, the policy makers of the state have failed to formulate a well-thought out Naxal policy to contain the spread of Naxal activities. Critics therefore alleged that, this alarming situation due to mostly designed by 'no Naxal policy' of the state. Successive state governments, over the years have not been able to come out with a police to win over its own people from the Naxals nor did they effectively used force to suppress the extremist activities. Of course the state government has clamped a ban on the Naxal outfits since 2006. But a ban itself is not a solution. The surrender and rehabilitation package of Naxals so far has failed to give deprivation, exploitation, land alienation and socio-economic discrimination etc. are the prime reasons identified by scholars for the spread of extremists in Orissa.

CONCLUSION

Naxalite movement has raised several important questions regarding rights, liberty and livelihood of the downtrodden people of Orissa. It has also underlined the need to bring about equality and equally in the society- the verson which has been enshrined in the Indian Constitution. But over the years the policy makers have failed to understand the entrinsic problems of Naxalite movement. While the political leadership called it is a law and order problem, the bureaucrats believed it as a socio-economic problem. But debate between law and order problem and relative deprivation must be ended. Since Naxalite movement has posed socio-economic, political and security challenges, it should be understood in a broader perspective and multifaceted long term approach should be adapted to solve the problem. Studies have revealed that there is direct correlation between poverty, exploitation and Naxalism. Hence, the following appropriate measures should be undertaken to tackle Naxal menace in the State.

1. Politically, the state should strengthen its governing system at the grass root level-it must ensure that its institutions do not breed exploitation. It should remain accountable, and responsible to people's needs and demands. The State must work on a formula where there is larger democratic participation of the people in the process of decision making and development. Three-tier Panchayati Raj bodies should be strengthened to ensure better delivery system. State must strengthen its judicial mechanism in the rural areas to resolve say to day conflicts. Nyaya Panchayat institutions should be established in the Naxalite infested areas to provide simple and inexpensive justice.

2. Social infrastructure should be strengthened in the Naxalite areas. The state must sufficiently increase and manage fund allocation properly in the field of health care, education, nutrition programme, social security measures, disease control, irrigation, rural electrification, rural road and other basic requirements in the backward areas. Mass awareness campaigns) padayatra, Jana Samparka Yatra) should be organized by the local authorities, political parties and other civil society based organization to restore confidence among the tribals and downtrodden people. People's elected representatives need to build public opinion against the extremist activities.

3. Expansion of economic activities in Naxalite affected areas is the key to normalize the situation. Generation of gainful employment opportunities in the backward areas is the best measure to contain the extremist activities. The state must ensure that the benefits of various employment and other schemes in vogue such as the Rural Employment Guarantee Schemes, Pradhan Mantri Sadak Yojana, Indira Awas Yojana etc. should reach to common people. Financial assistance in terms of small loans and creation of self help groups in the tribal areas is among other measures which need to be strengthend in Naxal areas. There is also need of strengthening local marketing system in the tribal areas. Adivasi Hatas (Weekly Markets) should be upgraded and forest produce should be provided a fixed minimum support price for various commodities.

4. Land issue continues a vital reason for expansion of Naxalite activities in Orissa to solve the problem: (i) Land Tribunals of Fast Track Courts (Article 323(B) of Constitution should be establish for quick

disposal of land ceiling cases; (ii) the tenancy laws should suitably amended to carter the needs of the tenancy; (iii) Laws relating transfer of Adivasi land to non Adivasi should be amended; (iv) Land reform measures should be given priority and surplus land should be allotted to landless poor people.

5. Autonomy and control over resources should be handed over to tribal communities so that they can enjoy the benefits. Further, mineral rules should be amended transferring all queries with annual leases values up to 10 lakhs to Gram Sabha and Gram Panchayats to cover all mines and mineral resources.

6. Policing is a principle for restoring normalcy in extremist infested areas. A number of measures should be undertaken by state for improving policing at the Naxalite areas. The state should modernize police force and upgrade police department to tackle the Naxalite menace. Given the unusual conflict dynamics of the Naxalite activities, police force should be provided with anti-guerrilla training and equipped with sophisticated weapons. Police should understand the changing Naxal activities, [perception and operation. Building and intelligence network is therefore, another important aspect of police modernization. Besides, social policing of communal policing system should be strengthening in Naxalite areas to build an intelligence network at the grass root level. (Bhanslae:2007)

7. Since Orissa is a part of 'Common war zone', a well coordinate Naxal Policy should be adopted among the affected states. Besides inter-state coordination mechanism, the central government must play a vital role to contain and control Naxal menace.

8. Last but not least, instead of banning the Naxalite outfits, they should be invited to participate in peace dialogue. Special attention should be given by the state to bring back the extremists to the main stream of society.

At the end, we may conclude that Naxalite movement is one of the greatest challenges of our nation building. But through enlightened development policy, proper execution, expansion of governance and well thought out security measures this extremist challenges can be overcome.

REFERENCES

Banarjee, B.L., 2006, "Maoist Movement in India-Bengal Naxalbari", *Economic and Political Weekly*, July, 22, 2006, pp. 3154-3163.

Bandopadhya, D, (2007), Naxalism-Rural Unrest, Yojana, Vol. 51, February 2007, pp. 11-14.

Bhansle, R.K., (2007), Naxalism-an Integrated Strategy, Yojana, Vol. 51, February 2007, pp. 31-35.

Financial Express, 18th February, 2008.

Forest War, *Down to Earth*, Dec. 31, 2001, New Delhi, p. 33-35.

Frontline, 'a Naxalite Corridor, Vol. 22, Issue 14, July 02-15, 2005.

Gupta, T.D, (2006), Maoism in India-Ideology, Programme and Armed Struggle, *Economic and Political Weekly*, July 22, 2006, pp. 3172-3176.

Jha, S.K, Naxalite Consolidation in Orissa, *South Asia Intelligence Review*, Vol. 2, No. 3, August 4, 2003.

Kujur, R.K., (2007), Naxal Movement and its Conflict Dynamics", *Human Touch,* Vol. IV, No. 4, April, 2007, pp. 16-17.

Mahanty, M, (2006) "Challenges of Revolutionary Violence-The Naxalite Movement in Perspective", *Economic and Political Weekly*, July, 22, 2006, pp. 3163-3168.

Mahanty, M, (1977), *The Revolution and Violence: A Study of the Maoist Movement in India*, New Delhi.

Mehera, A.K., 2007, "Naxalism-India's Gordian Knot", *Yojana*, Vol. 51, February, 2007, pp. 37-40.

Naxalism-The Problem, *Yojana*, Vol. 51, February, 2007, pp. 5-7.

Naxal Movement as Developmental Challenge: *A Review Report of the Planning Commission: A Human Touch*, Vol. 5, No. 6, June 2008, pp. 14-15.

Pioneer, Editorial (2006) in Frontline Protest, June 21.

Singh, M., 2007, Naxalism-Issues and Concerns, *Yojana*, Vol. 51, February, 2007, pp. 9-10.

The Hindu, 15th April 2006, New Delhi.

The Telegraph, "Report Sound ISI Alarm, September 21, Kolkata, 2004.

The Times of India, 29th June, Bhubaneswar, 2008.

The Times of India, 7th October, Bhubaneswar, 2008.

7

UNEASY CALM AT NAYAGARH

Dr. Uddipan Mukherjee

It was probably any other day at Nayagarh. People were carrying on their daily chores as usual. Workers returned to home at dusk. Hardly the children or the aged or the women folk were aware of the thunderbolt that was going to strike the area, or did they know? Whatever it was, the upshot is that the night of 15th February, 2008 remains a memorable one for the Nayagarh-ites and would continue to be so. Not unlike any commercial thriller, the Maoists pillaged the Police stations in the area, looted a huge cache of arms and ammunition and also killed the Assistant Sub-Inspector Dandapani Mishra. They had arrived in large numbers, about 500-600 in total, in trucks and on motorcycles.

Now in what way is this assault of the Maoists unique that it requires a threadbare analysis? Moreover, keeping in mind the plethora of attacks they have had launched over the past five years, this one at Nayagarh might not be that pertinent to be ascribed so much importance; especially, after such dramatic events like that in Koraput in 2004 or the Jehanabad jail break in 2005. Agreed that such events or even the assassination bid on Chandrababu Naidu would be considered notches up in terms of intensity or ferocity, but the issue which warrants special attention here is the proliferation of the Maoists in the interior of Orissa.

And that has to be given due recognition. It is a fact that the Red Corridor passes through Orissa, but the border districts such as Gajapati, Rayagada, Koraput and Malkanagiri in the south and Deogarh, Sundargarh, Jharsuguda and Sambalpur in the north are mostly affected. Penetrating so deep into the heartland not only speaks volumes of the military success of the Maoists but also signify their expanding socio-political network in the region. Moreover, the casual approach of the local administration along with the failure of their espionage system have to be held responsible for this ominous incident.

Starting from the deadly mine attack on the then Andhra Pradesh Chief Minister Chandrababu Naidu in 2003, the Maoists have thus come far in terms of their reach and military prowess. Or it may be that they are trying to create a notion in the mind of the administration regarding their penetrative abilities by embarking on sudden guerilla attacks on towns away from their core areas. Nevertheless, the Nayagarh event was startling and it was one among the series of such field actions of the Maoists which they are carrying out with élan since the camaraderie that they achieved after the unification of the two erstwhile warring factions : Maoist Communist Centre (MCC) and People's War Group (PWG) in late 2004; a decisive moment in the history of the Naxalite movement in India.

It all began in March 1967 with a young share-cropper Bigul Kisan, in the Naxalbari area being attacked by armed goons of the local jotedar when he had gone to till the land after having a judicial order. Oppression was thwarted by arms, autocracy of the landlord-bourgeoisie nexus was bludgeoned by a unified band of tribal-peasants : invigorated by the fiery speeches of the cult-figure Charu Mazumdar. Since then, the movement has seen several ups and downs, bitter internecine showdowns, severe State repressions as well as splits, mergers and a Mega-merger. But the central theme of the Naxalites has remained almost the same. They have viewed independent India as a multi-national country and supported the right of nationalities to self-determination, including secession. Moreover, they have clearly stated that the ruling bourgeoisie is comprador, Indian independence was fake, and that India has a semi-colonial and semi-feudal status. Thus, in order to establish a people's government in India, Mao Zedong's guerilla warfare tactics have to be employed and a protracted armed agrarian revolution is the only feasible solution in this regard.

Coming back to Nayagarh on the eventful night of 15th February, it would hardly be necessary to solve intricate mathematical equations to predict the future security calculus of the region. Nayagarh is strategically close to the pilgrim site of Puri in the south-east and the capital Bhubaneswar in the north-east. In fact, it was carved out of the Puri district itself in 1995. Thus a full-scale Maoist offensive on Nayagarh would act as an apparition for the nearby districts. Moreover, the incident can also have a debilitating effect on the influx of tourists to Puri. Furthermore, attacks of this class can stem the inflow of FDI (Foreign Direct Investment) in future. Given the predilection of the Maoists towards foreign capital and POSCO's venture at Paradip, a port barely 120 km by road from Bhubaneswar; such a hypothesis cannot be ruled out. Apart from these, it is noteworthy that the civilian casualty was remarkably low (only one civilian was killed in the crossfire). The Naxalites, as they entered the area, kept on warning the locals regarding the coming tussle and requested them to stay indoors. The modus-operandi is similar to what they had adopted in such mass operations elsewhere. This goes to show that the Maoists are trying to establish themselves as an organization against the oppressive State machinery and not against the masses. They are determined to remove the 'terrorist' tag. Also, it is natural that a closer contact with the masses would help the Maoists to engineer the economy of the area. The sugarcane cultivation in the region may be the focal point of attraction for the Maoists.

Hence the State and the Union administration have started to act in unison to weed out the menace before it assumes cyclopean proportions. Indeed they have to, before it becomes too late. But to only consider the Maoist problem as an administrative hindrance would be myopic. Unless the tribals and peasants are properly empowered, the Naxalite problem would persist. The top rebel leader Sabyasachi Panda: the chief architect of Maoism in Orissa since 1996, belongs to the town. Well, he has a number of admirers in the political circles of Orissa !! Before Sabyasachi Panda of Nayagarh establishes himself in the annals of Indian History as a legendary figure, the administration has to assert itself, though not in the manner of "Salwa Judum" in Chhattisgarh. Till then, an uneasy calm prevails at Nayagarh and in Orissa.

8

NAXALISM
NEED OF A SOCIO-ECONOMIC SOLUTION

Dr. Dasarathi Bhuyan

The major concern of today's India is internal security. The country confronts a wide range of complex internal security problems and threats. The government of India has admitted now that 160 districts are affected by Naxalites converting them into "Liberation Zones" and taking upon themselves the functions of the state administration and police. Naxalism is seen as the single largest internal security challenges ever faced by the country. Of the 13 affected States, the movement is intense in parts of Chhattisgarh, Jharakhand, Orissa, Madhya Pradesh, Maharashtra, while it making inroads in Kerala, Karnataka, Tamilnadu, Uttarakhand and Haryana. The Naxal problem is not merely a law and order problem, it needs to be dealt with as a socio-economic problem. The Naxalites will continue to breed internal unrest and upset peace till such time the economic inequalities are not addressed. The down trodden poor, unprivileged classes of the society are mostly concentrated in the Naxal activities. Unless their grievances are addressed speedily, their resentment can not be pacified.

ORIGIN OF NAXALISM

Even after two decades of India's independence, a large segment of the Indian population - peasants, workers and tribals - continued to suffer the worst forms of exploitation. They thought that a peaceful rather corrupt political process would not solve their problem. Therefore, they considered an armed struggle was the only option. This attitude of these depressed classes was the genesis of Naxalism in India.

The Naxalite movement derives its name from a small village Naxalbari on the tri-junction of India, Nepal and what was then East Pakistan, where tribals took up arms against the oppression of the landlords in 1967. The movement spread like wildfire to different parts of the country. Some of the finest brains and the cream of India's youth in certain areas left their homes and colleges to chase the dream of a new world, a new social order. (Prakash Singh: Naxal Movement in India).

An account of the insurgent activities begins with the Naxalite movement in the late 1960s under the leadership of Charu Mazumdar. A section of ultra-leftist left the Communist Party of India-Marxist and on the 100th birth of Lenin (22 April, 1969) formed their own organization with the name of Communist Party of India (Marxist-Leninist). Taking inspiration from the experiment of China under the leadership of Mao, Charu declared that 'China's Chairman is our Chairman.' He issued shrill calls for annihilation of class enemies. It led to the murder of petty landlords, sharecroppers, money-Landers and government officers. In not much time the people felt disillusioned with the dictates of Charu mazumdar and Kanu Sanyal. After the death of Charu Mazumdar on 28 July 1972, the movement lost momentum. It had its manifestation in the states of Andhra Pradesh, Bihar and Kerala also. Originally Naxalism was based on the theory of class struggle of Karl Marx. Actually long back in China Mao Tse-tung established socialism through democratic revolution with a huge mass support. Theoretically he applied Marxism and Leninism in the communist to the needs of an overwhelmingly agricultural and still traditional society. Indian Naxalities accept Maoism (It is usually understood as an anti-bureaucratic form of Marxism that places its faith in the radical zeal of the masses) at the ideological level but their strategies and methods of revolt unlike Maoist theory. In fact, Naxalism in India is an ideological, political and economic struggle to establish economic, social and political equality and abolish any kind of exploitation in the society. The emergence of peasant resistance by Santhal tribals in a village of Naxalbari in West Bengal in the decade of 1960 later on known as Naxalities movement in 1967. The Naxalbari uprisings of March 1967 saw the implementation of Charu Majumdar's vision of revolution "Expand anywhere and everywhere".

The tribals of Naxalbari, armed with bows and arrows, forcibly occupied the land of kulaks and ploughed them to establish their ownership. Demonstrations were organized against persons holding paddy in their godowns. In many cases, the entire stocks were lifted and distributed or sold locally to the poor peasants at cheaper rates. For this act of the rebels there were violent clashes between the haves and have-nots in the society. Between March and May 1967, nearly a hundred incidents were reported to the police. The situation progressively deteriorated. After some dithering, the West Bengal government ordered the police to take action. The movement was squashed, but "Naxalbari exploded many a myth" (Prakash Singh: Naxal Movement in India).

Charu Majumdar who led the movement is known as the father of Naxalism. The ultra-leftist ideology took a concrete shape at May 1968 meeting of All India Coordination Committee of Communist Revolutionaries (AICCCR) which represented revolutionaries from seven states of Tamil Nadu, Kerala, Uttar Pradesh, Bihar, Karnataka, Orissa and West Bengal. In 1969, Communist Party (Marxist-Leninist) was formed under the leadership Charu Majamudar. It argued that democracy in India was pretense and decided to base Indian revolution on protracted guerrilla warfare on the lines of Chinese Model. There were three announced mottos of Naxal movement. These are: (1) To provide the land right to the peasants; (2) Abolish the foreign capital power; and (3) to struggle against the class and caste. However, the famous 1970 programme of CPI (ML) projected an understanding that a strong worker-peasant alliance and effective implementation of Mao's theory can help revolutionaries to defeat powerful enemies like big landlords, bureaucrats, capitalists and government, which is a "lackey of US imperialism and Soviet Social Imperialism". The Chinese Communist party welcomed the formation of the CPI (ML). The Marxist-Lenisist groups of other countries like UK, Albania and Srilanka also extended their recognition (Prakash Singh: Naxal Movement).

THE RISE

The Naxalite movement, drawing inspiration from the Maoist ideology, had a meteoric phase for about two years from the formation of the party till the end of June 1971. The ripples starting from Naxalbari spread in ever-widening circles to particularly all parts of the country. It was viewed as a "higher form of class struggle and the beginning of guerrilla war". Charu's assessment was that "every corner of India is like a volcano" about to erupt, that: "there is the possibility of a tremendous upsurge in India", and he therefore called upon the cadres to start as many points of armed struggle as possible. "Expand anywhere and everywhere" was his message. Such expansions were particularly noticeable in Srikakulam in Andhra Pradesh, Debra-Gopiballavapur in west Bengal, Mushahari in Bihar, and Palia in Laxmipur district of U.P.

The political parties realized the emergence of a new force. The government became conscious of a new threat not only to law and order but to very existence of the democratic structure of the country.

Naxal activities occurred in a part of Assam under the leadership of A.Z. Phizo who talked about an independent state of Nagaland. But after his escape to Nagaland in 1956, the movement became weak and with the creation of the state of Nagaland in 1963 it failed. But Manipur and Tripura became the center of such activities. In Manipur the Meitis created serious problems by taking to the course of insurgent. When the Prepak Chief (R.K. Tulachand Singh), who carried a reward of Rupees 50,000 on his head, was arrested by the Central Reserve Police Force, the Armed Guard of Manipur Rifles let him escape. The situation was made more complicated by the Chief Minister of the Congress, Rajkumar Dorendra Singh who issued the call of 'back to Sanamahi' implying abandonment of the faith of Hinduism and instead to the centuries old meiti faith implying recall of the Mongolian past. Thus enthused, the Meitis raised the demand for the deportation of the 'Mayangs' (foreigners) from their state. The violent mobs burnt down hundreds of the huts and scores of motor vehicles of the 'outsiders' on 28 April 1980 in the city of Imphal and forced to flee for saving their life. The situation grew more complicated when the Nationalist Socialist Council of Nagaland (NSCN) retaliated the Meiti rebels for saving the life of the Nagas living there.

The non-tribal became the target of the militant tribals in Tripura who formed their own organization called Tripura *Upjati Juba Samiti*. In June 1980 the extremists butchered about 300 Bengalis in the Mandari Bazar of Agartala. The organization of the Tripura National Volunteers (TNV) led by Bijoy Harankhal and supported by Bangladesh as well as by the hostile Mizos is playing its own part in this regard. Apart from killing the security forces and the non-tribals, these elements collect levies regularly from the leaders, contractors and public servants. Though the problems of the Mizos could be solved with creation of the state of Mizos and, the hostile elements of the Mizo National Front continued their activities, some of them being in league with the TNV. The people of Bodo community in Assam have come forward with the demand for their own with the name of Bodoland and their violent activities under the leadership of Biswamutari and Brahma in the area of Kokrajhar may be referred to this connection.

Trends of Overall Naxal Violence

Head	*2002*	*2003*	*2004*	*2005*	*2006(31.10.2006)*
No. of Incidents	1465	1597	1533	1608	1272
Police Personnel Killed	100	105	100	158	129
Civilians Killed	382	410	466	519	481
Naxalites Killed	414	216	87	223	210

The formation of People's War Group in Andhra Pradesh subsequently in 1980 under the leadership of Kondapalli Seetharamaiah gave a new lease of life to the movement. The PWG is believed to have redistributed nearly half of a million acres of land across Andhra Pradesh. Its activities also insisted on a hike in the daily minimum wages and the annual fee for jeetagadu(year long labour). The poorer sections found that what the politicians had been talking about and the government promising year after year could be translated into a rewality only with the intervention of Naxalites. Kidnapping to secure the realese of its own cadres was frequently resorted to by the PWG activities. The Andhra Pradesh government banned the PWG and its six front organizations in 1992. (Prakash Singh, p. 25).

Naxal Violence in Andhra Pradesh

Head	*2002*	*2003*	*2004*	*2005*
No. of Incidents	346	577	310	532
Police Personnel Killed	12	12	06	47
Civilians Killed	84	127	68	184
Naxalites Killed	87	163	4715	160

Source: Ministry of Home Affairs.

In Bihar, the Maoist Communist Centre, another major Naxalite formation, perpetrated acts of violence. Its organizational network extended to most of the Central Bihar districs. There were major incidents in Gaya, Chapra, and Aurangabad districts in which Rajputs, Bhumihars and

Muslims policemen were killed. What began as a fight for social and economic justice actually degenerated into a caste conflict with a veneer of class struggle. The MCC ran virtually a parallel judiciary system in certain pockets. These were described as Jana Adalats or People's Court where they would even shorten an acuused by six inches-behead him, in other words. (Prakash Singh, p. 26).

Naxal Violence in Bihar

Head	*2002*	*2003*	*2004*	*2005*
No. of Incidents	239	250	323	183
Police Personnel Killed	06	26	95	24
Civilians killed	11	102	166	70
Naxalites Killed	22	09	01	10

Source: Ministry of Home Affairs.

Lately, the Maoist Communist Centre has shifted its focus to the Jharkhand region, which was carved out of Bihar on November 15, 2000. The Naxalites are said to be active in 15 out of the 22 districts of Jharkhand. They have been particularly targeting the police and the paramilitary personnel. (Prakash Singh, p, 27).

Naxal Violence in Jharkhand

Head	*2002*	*2003*	*2004*	*2005*
No. of Incidents	353	342	379	308
Police Personnel Killed	63	16	41	27
Civilians killed	94	101	128	91
Naxalites Killed	13	21	20	07

Source: Ministry of Home Affairs.

In Madhya Pradesh, following the bifurcation of the state in November 2000, Naxalite violence is now confined to Balghat, Mandla, Dindori, and Sidhi districts. In Chhattisgarh, Naxlite violence is concerned mainly in Bastar area and in Rajnandagaon, Jagadlpur, Jashpur and Sarguja districts. The state government has been trying to mobilize the tribals through 'Salwa Judam' (peace Mission). This is being vehemently opposed by the Naxlites and they have been recklessly killing the Judam activists. (Prakash Singh, p. 27)

Naxal Violence in Chhattisgarh

Head	*2002*	*2003*	*2004*	*2005*
No. of Incidents	304	256	352	380
Police Personnel Killed	9	30	08	47
Civilians killed	46	44	75	118
Naxalites Killed	10	08	15	32

Source: Ministry of Home Affairs.

Orissa witnessed a qualitative increase in Naxalite violence after 2000. The MCC has established its presence in the northern districts while PWG has consolidated its hold over the southern districts. The formation of Andhra-Orissa Border special Zonal committee gave fillip to Left wing Extremism in the State.

Naxal Violence in Orissa

Head	*2002*	*2003*	*2004*	*2005*
No. of Incidents	68	49	352	380
Police Personnel Killed	07	12	04	01
Civilians killed	04	03	04	13
Naxalites Killed	01	01	00	03

Source: Ministry of Home Affairs.

Uttar Pradesh has witnessed stirring on Naxalite activities in the eastern belt in Sonbhadra, Gorakhpur, Ghazipur, Ballia, Candauli and Mirzapur districts. In Maharashtra, Gadchiroli is particularly affected, though there are incidents in Bhandara, Chandrapur, Gondia and Naded districts also. In Karnataka, Naxalites have been active in Kudermukh area following government's move to evict the tribals from the forests. (Prakash Singh, p. 27).

Naxal Violence in Maharashtra

Head	*2002*	*2003*	*2004*	*2005*
No. of Incidents	83	75	84	95
Police Personnel Killed	03	08	06	24
Civilians killed	26	23	09	29
Naxalites Killed	00	09	02	03

Source: Ministry of Home Affairs.

SIDETRACKED IDEOLOGY

Even though, it is a different thing to be analyzed that Naxal movement was started in the beginning to defend underprivileged, deprived and poor people's benefits. However, afterward it has sidetracked from its sole object. In reality these days Naxalism is a different name for frightening ordinary populace, obstructing harmony, peace, and spoiling law and order in more than half states of the country.

In the beginning the Naxal movement was launched to safeguard the interests of the economically underprivileged people who had to bear the atrocities of the rich landlords following strong genuine reasons but with the passive of time the movement seems to have converted into an anti-social problem. How can Naxalism provide social equality by indulging in kidnapping, killing of police personnel and thereby creating fear and unrest in general public? It is argued that Naxal movement gets its strength from being the champion of the cause of the poor and the oppressed, but violence in society will always dealt with punishment by the state machinery. Investigation reveal that Naxalities are involved in illicit narcotic trade and smuggling of counterfeit Indian currency. The Naxalities have a very well knit organizational structure and have a pan-India strategy. They aim to control the economic resources of the region and operation in areas rich in natural resources like minerals, Tendu Patta, Katha Trees, etc. Besides terrorizing the local populace and traders, the Naxalites have also resorted to extortion. The Naxalites leadership continues to pursue its plan to wage a protracted people's war through the armed struggle to capture political power. They seem to lay greater focus on organizing along military lines. Their constant effort is to upgrade their weaponry. Regular cadre recruitment is carried out. And now schools are being the latest focus of attention. Their aim here is to create "Bal Dasta" or Child squads. (Alka R Gupta, *The Naxal Problem - Need for Good Governance*)

CAUSES OF NAXALISM

Many scholars believe that for the rise of Naxalism in India mainly the socio-economic factors are responsible. It is true that Naxalites got inspiration for their growth from China but India's social, political and economic conditions forced them to develop. After the independence various programmes introduced for the rural area development. But due to feudal nature of the authority, complex, rules and regulations, corrupt, administrative dullness and the lack of general awareness like causes, the real benefit of development process limited within few selfish groups and people. (Alka R. Gupta, The Naxal Problem - Need for Good Governance).

Fifty-eight per cent of the Indian labour force is still engaged in agricultural and allied occupations. Tribals are being pushed up the hills because of illegal incursion of outsiders in their traditional domain. Dalits continue to swell the ranks of agricultural proletariat which is increasing in an alarming way. Poverty ratio among the Scheduled Castes and Scheduled Tribes continue to be much higher at 35 per cent and 44.2 per cent respectively as against the national average of little over 26 per cent. Neo-liberal development process totally by-passed them. Not only that the invasion of the corporate sector into agriculture and forestry and enhancement of ceiling limits on land in some states has exacerbated the incidence of landlessness with the consequential rise in the free floating mass of the rural poor moving around in search of employment. This has depressing effect on rural wages and has aggravated causalisation of labour on terms grossly unfavorable to them. This is supported by different rounds of NSSO data on agricultural wage from 1983 to 2000. (D.Bandopadhyay: *Rural Unrest*)

Victims of development - the project affected people (PAP)-add another unpleasant dimension to the scenario of rural alienation and turmoil. The generally accepted figure (calculated by Walter Fernandese) is that between 1951 and 2005, about 50 to 60 million persons were forcibly evicted from their hearth and home. Thus a vast number of displaced, homeless, landless and jobless tribals are roaming about as flotism and jetsam of the cruel development process. They are depressed and dejected, irritated and angry.

Extension of general laws and their accompanying institutions to the Scheduled Tribal areas created a hiatus between the "modern" laws and their agencies and the traditional mode of tribal life and living style. This resulted in a conflict between the traditional systems and formal institutions, especially with regard to the rights of the tribal people over land and resources on which they had subsisted for centuries without formal ownership deed or title. This crisis has been further aggravated by influx of individuals and corporate bodies into the tribal domain and their take over of tribal lands and other natural resources which traditionally gave sustenance to tribals.

The tribals lost their control of traditional livelihood resources through several state actions. First is the forest reservation policy which declared forests, degraded forests, waste lands on the periphery and even partly arable lands as reserved forests where human habitation was prohibited. These reserved areas sometimes included villages which were allowed to continue without any right or title and which supplied free or cheap labour to forest Department and/to forest personnel. The second means of alienation was the leasing of forest lands to the corporate sector for mining, processing industries, agricultural or forest based business, logging and timber felling or for tourism venture. Thirdly there were draconian laws regarding wild life protection and national parks and sanctuaries which forcefully excluded all habitations from vast areas notified under these laws.

Displacement of tribals turned them homeless, landless, resourcesless and jobless. Therefore, social unrest has emerged in the affected areas. It manifests itself in defiance of the authority from simple form of demanding right of community management of forests to militancy. (D. Bandopadhyay: *Rural Unrest*)

Moreover, the policies of LPG (Liberalization, Privatization and Globalization) initiated in 1991 acknowledged the social-economic inequality as the binding part of development process. The State's anti-poverty programmes such as the NDA's food-for-work or the UPA's Employment Guaranteee Programme hardly meet the basic demand for land rights in rural India. The rise of backward castes to power in Bihar, Uttar Pradesh and elsewhere, even though it may have democratized certain aspects of the polity, has had the paradoxical effect of freezing land relations. All these have kept the Naxal agenda alive. (Alka R Gupta, *The Naxal Problem - Need for Good Governance)*

COUNTER NAXAL STRATEGIES

Given the constitutional diversity in law and order between the state and the centre, it has not been possible to follow a uniform strategy. As the overall strategy of the Naxals is well coordinated, the fallout of varied policies by different states is invariably castigated. There are reasons to belive however that it may be possible to follow divergent strategies between states and even within different districts in a state depending on the level of militancy, the level of their operations. There is no doubt that this will create situations where Naxalite under pressure in one district may seek sanctuary in other areas, but it has the benefit of winning over local support by establishing a positive differential. (R.K.Bhonsle: *An Integrated Strategy*).

The primary strategy selected has to be people centric rather than the normal trend of terrorist focus. The variation is subtle and thus needs deliberation. In people centric strategies, all activities law and order, development of humanitarian are related to providing relief to the people, be it immediate, short and ling term. Operations impinging on safety and security of the public are avoided even if it implies a temporary reprieve to the militants. The example of Salwa Judam could perhaps highlight this facet. The displacement of almost 70,000 people from their homes and livelihood has possibly occurred as the larger implications of such a movement and its Naxalite backlash was not realized. Today it has become an example of living human tragedy, where poor tribal have been made refugees in their own homeland. The people-centric strategies does not imply a pacific approach to contrary it would entail search and destroy missions seeking out the guerillas but avoiding fall out of the confrontation on the masses. (R.K.Bhonsle: *An Integrated Strategy*)

Two approaches could be adopted for the control of Naxalism. Negotiation with the local Naxal leadership, which may not work initially, but if persisted could achieve results and could be attempted. The other option is to neutralize the Naxals, for which at present, operations by the army appear to be the only alternative. Operations in this area will be perforce control and neutralize influence of terrorists. Situational protection of a wide variety of targets will be essential. Police will have to be supported by special commando taskforces based on Greyhound model of Andhra Pradesh Concomitantly follow up development operations are essential. These operations need to be developed heavy, limiting police influence to creating an atmosphere of safety and security for conduct of normal economic activities. A broken windows approach has to be followed in that even the smallest incident has to be investigated and the culprits nailed. (R.K.Bhonsle: *An Integrated Strategy*)

Reestablishing grassroots governance implies ensuring that benefits of various schemes in vogue such as the rural employment guarantee scheme. Pradhan Mantri Gram Sadak Yojana, the security related expenditure grants reach the "Aam Admi" rather than remaining grandiose proclamations blared from the rampant of festooned daises. This will necessitate major organizational changes in our delivery mechanisms and attitudes from the lowest patwaris, Naib tahasildars, tehsidars to the key to all governance, the district magistrate. In parallel, people's representatives need to build public opinion to support the executive. (R.K.Bhonsle: *An Integrated Strategy*)

Selected District Magistrates and Superintendent of Police preferably volunteers should be posted to these districts for a minimum tenure of three years. No post in the district administration should be left vacant and special monetary as well as promotion incentive should be provided to officials, who will be functioning under extreme threat of danger to life.

Volunteers for serving in these districts could be called for, alternatively two year tenure should be made mandatory before grant of next promotion at all levels and additional bonus in terms of financial and monetary benefits could be granted.

A coordinated grid comprising of security and administration incorporating all elements of the society has to be established. The role of the grid will be two fold, containment of the root causes and symptoms of militancy and expanding effectiveness of governance. (R.K.Bhonsle, *An Integrated Strategy*).

It is a fact that Naxalism rampant in some parts of the country can be effectively checked by means of stringent legislative measures and effective administrative action. It is equally necessary to check the prevalence of corruption and lethargy in functioning of the Central and State governments. In many cases, paramilitary forces could not succeed in their mission owing to the links of the Naxals with local people and other echelons of administration. What should there fore, be done? It is always a disaster to regard insurgency a military problem and hand it over to the army. It is primarily an administrative and an emotional problem. It is better to use paramilitary forces trained in internal security and working under a civil administration. Development should never be pushed into the background; one has to convince the people that they have more to gain by this method than by adding and harbouring the insurgents. There must be a first intelligence and paramilitary set up to ensure that external aid does not reach the insurgents. In those areas whenever there is an internal conflict between the people and vested interest group, the government should side with the people. Naxalism should be fought effectively because the people can have no faith in a government, which cannot protect them. Many groups of people have become marginalized over the years as a consequence of both democracy and development and they have to be brought back to the national mainstream. Educational and employment opportunities must be provided to them. As a first step towards getting rid of Naxal terror menace uninhibited brainstorming is the appropriate activity at this stage. On the basis of such mutual discussions and interlocutions, critical analysis of current policies to deal with Naxalism can take place.

Mere deliberations, slogan mongering, path Yatras and fashions of panel discussions on media will not resolve this problem. The cause of frustration and anger in the societies is manifold like: poverty, illiteracy, deprivation of basic human rights, unemployment, humiliation of the people, wrong policies of the government, and white-collar-crime committed by the upper strata of our societies in their business and professional practices like tax evading, black marketing, racketeering, public corruption, bribes by responsible officers and so on. The time comes when this accumulated frustration and anger explodes in the form of a violence to show resentment against these oppressions and repressions. The resources allotted for the programmes of poverty alleviation are not reaching the poor masses but are miss-utilized and defalcated by the elites with the connivance of the authorities. This larceny is widening the gap between the poor and the rich and if this disparity is not bridged, it will undoubtedly unleash more Naxalism in the various societies of the world In order to tackle the menace of Naxalism, we have to tackle those fundamental issues first, which give rise to this evil.

The changes in character and style of the Naxal movement must be recognized. There is growing militarization and superior army-style organization. This needs strengthening of local policing and intelligence gathering system. Competent officer's need to be posted in the Naxilite affected districts and areas with stable tenure. "Greyhounds" of Andhra Pradesh can serve as model to other affected states. Winning the confidence of local population is another important area. In several meetings called by the centre of affected states, it has emerged that the drives against movement have often been by the lack of coordination between states and central intelligence agencies. The positive outcome of these meetings has been that the Centre has now made it clear that it will closely monitor the implementation of counter-revolutionary strategies in different states. Earlier the Union Government's role was confined to sending paramilitary forces, reimbursing security related expenditure to States and modernization of police. But, recently the Central government has been focusing on reducing the sense of deprivation and alienation among the underprivileged classes. Time has come to check the inroads of Naxalism into the tribal areas and allow fruits of economic development to reach faster to the affected areas.

REFERENCES

Alka R. Gupta, The Naxal Problem - Need for Good Governance, *South Asia Politics*, New Delhi, November 2007, p. 37-41.

D.Bandopadhyay, Rural Unrest, *Yojana*, February, 2007, pp. 11-14.

Indian Express, Bhubaneswar, December 14, 2007.

Indian Express, 23 February 2007.

J.C. Johari, *Terrorism, Indian Political System*, Anmol Publication, New Delhi, 1996, p. 315.

Manmohan Singh, Issues and Concerns, *Yojana*, February, 2007, pp. 9-10.

Marvin S Scores, *Beyond Sovereignty, The challenge of Global Policy*, University of South Carolina Press, 1986, p, 93.

N.S. Saksena: *Terrorism: History and Facets in the World and in India*, Abhinav Publications, Delhi, 1985, p, 137.

Prakash Singh, Naxal Movement in Inda, *Yojana*, February, 2007, pp. 23-28.

Praveen Kumar, Terrorism - Some New Dimensions, in *Global Terrorism*, (Ed) B.P. Singh Sehagal, Deep and Deep, New Delhi, 1996, p. 74 .

R.K. Bhonsale, An Integrated Strategy, *Yojana*, February, 2007, pp. 31-36.

Sambad, Oriya Daily, Brahmapur Edition, 15 December, 2007.

S.R. Maheswari, *Terrorism in Politics, Comparative Government and Politics*, L.N. Agarwal, Agra, 1994, p. 183.

Yojana, February, 2007.

WWW.naxalwatch.com.

9

NAXAL MOVEMENT IN ORISSA

Dr. Bishnu Narayana Sethi

Human nature is very complex phenomenon and human relation on different levels have been characterized by decisions demonstrating the lasswellian method "Who gets what, when and how". Often accompanied by the threat and use of force. Political and ideological violence, which sometimes arises from and contribute to such conflict includes what is commonly known as "Naxalism'. It is also said that naxalist are not been but created by particulars, sociological, economic and political conditioning processes. Unless ordinary criminals naxalist are ostensively dedicated to some ideological cause.

During the past few decades, many opposition groups function groups functioning under different degrees of stress have intentionally utilised techniques of physically and psychological force which include intimidation, repulsion, coercion and destruction of property and lives for attaining ideological and political goals. It is this very agitational and destructive violence which is engaged in the process of destruction of norms that threaten many nations with disasters and has laid siege to our civilized world in an unprecedented way.

DEFINITION

Naxalism is not a recent phenomenon. It is older than the ancient civilization of Greece and Rome. Early examples include the assassination of Julius Caesar in 44 B.C. the example of serial, a religious sect. During the first century A.D. Zealot struggle in Palestine and the act of Secret.

Islamic armed bands in the twelfth and thirteenth centuries one of the earliest attempts to clarify the concept of Naxalism in modern social science defined it as-the method of theory whereby an organized group or party seeks to achieve its avowed aim chiefly through the systematic use of violence.

Another important attempt at the definition is of Thorntons whose definition includes symbolic character of naxalist acts. Therefore, Naxalism is a symbolic act intend to influence political behavior of a country by extra normal means entailing the use or threat of violence. The most important element in Thomton's definition is the claim that all act of naxal in an internal war are deliberately propagandist acts, which are always designed to convey a message sign or warning to either opponents the neutral population or to who belong to or sympathizes with the naxalist movement.

Therefore, it is clear that all kind of violence do not involve political Naxalism. But most act of violence such as wounding, arson, assassination, destruction of property etc. are defined as crimes under the legal codes of all states.

Arson, explosion flooding or submersion, ignition, flooding of asphyxiating or noxious substances,interruption of the normal operation of means of transport or communication, damage to or destruction of government property and public utilities. Population, fouling or deliberate, poisoning of drinking water or staple foods causing or propagating contagious or epidemic disease any willful act which endangers human lives and the community.

Grant Wardlaw defines political Naxalism as the use of violence by an individual or a group whether acting for or in opposition to established authority when such action is designed to create extreme anxiety or fear indicating effects in a target group larger then the immediate victims with the purpose of coercing that group into acceding to the political demands of the perpetrators.

Although individuals counter measures have been taken against the world is not yet in a position to eliminate this curse of human civilization. But perhaps the most important task is to find out the cause of Naxalism.

CAUSES

Misery, Zinism, Frustration, Fundamentalism, Racism, Political intolerance, Religion motivated, Crusades, Insecurity, Grievances and confusion both political and moral are growing in this world and contribute to psychological conditions for the increase of violence and Naxalism. States and governments are unable to agree how to arrest the escalation of violence which plung the society into chaos. The underlying reason for Naxalism is the political or economic interest of powerful groups. Who are in a possession of support the acts of Naxalism through powerful Govt. The linkages between domestic powers and processes with identical forces abroad are known as subsist.

The de-colonisation process has led to the formation of many mine and micro-sovereign states with population of million and less. This has resulted in stirring the ambitions of many small ethnic groups in various nations to recognize their separate identities and seek separate nationhood one of resultant consequences of such action retaliation by small developing nations against powerful nations in the form of state sponsored Naxalism.

TYPES OF VIOLENCE

Different type of violence are being spread in various sections and segments of the society. These are political , religious, educational and other social organization functioning in corporate way. All these institutions and organizations are integrated in a framework and primarily promote the main polices and programmes of the sponsoring state. The survival of many of these entities depend upon the recognition and patronage extended by the sponsoring state. Although there are various factors which are responsible for naxalism but many act of naxalism are the creation of a deeply ideological conviction or dedication to a certain political cause.

Both naxal and naxalism is also an outcome of many year of brutal suppression, physically torture and cultural dehumanization which is used by the colonial powers in a foreign country. In the process of ant-colonial struggle for national liberation, violence and naxalism become a necessary strategy. Naxalism is brought about where and when open political participation is not possible due to oppression.

The cause of naxalism are more or less the same unredressed grievances by the government, denial of legitimate political, economic and civil rights, frustration, because of unemployment, social and political injustice, naxalist do not respect the law or the normal rules of political conduct. In fact they look upon laws as unjust impositions and law-makers as usurpers and prejudicial people who some how manage to occupy the seats of power.

IDELOGY

Nevertheless despite these connections and causes of naxalism the struggle for liberation from foreign rule brings about another important dimension of naxalism which is systematically deployed by revolutionary leaders as an extension of guerrilla strategy. Almost in all the national liberation naxalism, guerrilla tactics played a very important role. But this does not mean the guerrilla warfare always employ naxalism, or even agree with the principle unless it is extremely and carefully supervised. It can rebound on the guerrillas by alienating the popular support which they depend upon. Sometimes naxalism gets provoked by security forces which could wipe out guerrilla calls and capture supplies which have been gathered over months of patient work of the revolutionaries.

Although naxals belong to different nationalities, religious, ideologies societies and ethinic groups they have certain things in common like dissatisfaction with the political setup. The use of unacceptable and illegal means to achieve certain goals which they consider legitimate some kind of ideology, behavior and motivation.

THE AIM AND OBJECTIVES

The aim of almost all categories of naxal is to pose a threat to those they consider oppressors, enemies and obstacles in the achievement of their goals. Their tactics include hijacking, black-mails, ruthless killing by shooting and use of bombs. Naxal groups are generally too small and weak to operate successfully against government. Therefore violence is not their immediate goal and that why they insist upon psychological rather then political results. The purpose of naxalism , therefore is to create an emotional state of extreme fear among specific groups and there by ultimately alter their behaviour and dispositions or being about general or particulars changes in the structures of society and government for example the aim of Palestinian naxals attacks in Jeruselam in 1975 was to gain popularity. Therefore naxals are generally dedicated to a cause for the achievement of which even the sacrifice of human life including their own lives are not considered important.

A successful naxals becomes a rebel, hero and a mastery. He wants to be an example for others. Although their act are criminal they become a sign of courage to be followed by the rest of group followers. Thus jostling crowds, busy hotels, crowded trains, water highway, country sides , even small and rural areas are increasingly becoming targets of modern naxals. The meek nature of the general masses at large has prevented cognate efforts by security forces to identify naxals immediately.

THE DANGER OF NAXAL MOVEMENT IN CONNECTION WITH RELIGION, IN ORISSA

The weeks-long Hindu Christian riots in Kandhamal District of Orissa is in connection with religion. In Orissa the riots are precipitated by the intensive, aggressive, extensive activities of hundred of fulltime, well-paid propagandists and agents. In Kandhamal District, alone there are 350 missionary organizations funded from all quarters of the world. They are engaging lots of unemployed people, to inveigle poor and uneducated Hindus into Christianity by monetary rewards, given in installments related to the number of people that these full-time markets of Christianity are able to convert. The fact that in Kandhamal District alone the Christian population has increased from 6 percent in 1970 to 27 percent in 2001, despite an Act enacted by Orissa Legislature in 1967 to prevent conversion shows the intensity of the multinational conversion enterprise marketing and financial clout.

In village after village, different denominations of Christians are planting Churches, recruiting converts as Pastors, paying them handsomely, they are also engaging thousands of unemployed Hindu youth for propagating Christianity and gaining converts. These are being rewarded in instalments. Just as the total compensation of company employees is having a fixed and varying components, fixed amount of varying amount related to the number of converts they are able to bring into Christianity.

It appears that they are telling the converts to continue to describe themselves as Hindu Scheduled Castes, so that they continue to get the benefit of reservations meant for Hindu SCs. They withhold the fact of conversion from the government records. At the same time in order to protect themselves from the exposure of fraud and continue to get benefit of reservation, they have launched a movement for get "Christian dalits". Almost all Hindus are feeling tremendously agitated about the intense activities of the multinational conversion enterprises, their planting of churches in Village. Families are getting divided, so are Village population and so will be the entire polity in state.

COMBATING STRATEGIES

For effective administrative measures, various sources of naxalism must be found first. There is a need for truly effective preparedness programmes at the government level. First of all we must know about the people involved in naxal activities and their motivation. The relationship dealing with naxal incident and mitigating its consequences need to be carefully thought out. Sufficient data about the area within which the event is unfold could be of immense use. This is simple work of good intelligence and police. The intelligence agencies should be able to provides the information about naxal targets timings and sites in advance. But government alone cannot do much to stop it. Individuals and groups can make a significant contribution towards improving the general security environment.

On the other hand there is a need for sophisticated security procedures which can go all the way airport screening to the border area. Some kind of positive programmes which can replace the frustration of naxal can prove effective. There is also a need to promote upon institutions, including political institution to absorb the ethnic, religious and political pressure and allow them to event their feelings in a proper way. This will change their mind and thus encourage them to settle their differences in some other way.

CONCLUSION

Since the present day naxals are very well organized and more professional then their counterparts a decade ago latest and modern techniques an procedure of safety and security should be introduce. A vigilant and assertive police and paramilitary network should replace the old one. Many of the important suggestions and recommendations of the various committees are not in tune with the existing circumstances. There is an apprehension that with the availability of biological and chemical weapons the naxals will start their campaign with renewed vigor and pursue their mission of destruction which will be virtually unstoppable. The role of intelligence and security force in naxal affected areas call for a multi-layered approach. But unless we attack at the roots of naxals, only an apparent relief will be seen and naxalism will increase in the total quantum of its impact.

At present it is impossible to clearly project the time and planning for wiping out naxalism. The current trends will be perricious with the course of heavy technology and weapons transfer. This threat can be encountered by training and development of a new mechanism bolstered up of a multi-dimensional and multiplayer approach based on checks and balances.

10

GROWTH OF NAXALISM AND PARTICIPATION OF WOMEN

Dr. Usha Padhy

The importance of peace can not be over estimated. One needs peace in mind, in house, in society, in country and in the whole world to live and grow in the real sense in a happy ambiance. Peace in society must depend upon the kind of society we live in; really progress is not possible unless there is peace.

Anti-social elements are the greatest threat to our country in the way of peace, because they undermine its stability. By creating chaotic conditions they derive enormous monetary gains from the perpetrators. In the present circumstances in India, there are certain elements inside the country who try to create instability and uncertainty. Some hostile neighbour countries want to disintegrate India because of India's eye catching economical growth.

The Supreme Court of India says, "Every organized criminal activity is an act of terrorism." In this context, Naxalism is an organized aggressive group creating internal disturbances in India. The apex court observed that "Naxalism is one of the manifestations of increased lawlessness and cult of violence which contribute a threat to an established order and a revolt against civilized and orderly society".

Naxalite is an informal name given to Communist groups who first started its attack in Naxalbari of West Bengal. A peasant was attacked by hired hands over a land dispute. Resulting, local peasants and tribals retaliated by attacking the local land lords and violence escalated. Charu Majumdar and Kanu Sanyal led the violent uprising in 1967 and tried to develop a revolutionary opposition to the CPI (Marxist) leadership. Majumdar greatly admired the attack and advocated that the Indian peasants, lower classes and tribals must follow the same step to overthrow the government and upper classes when he held responsible for their plight. He encouraged the Naxalite movement through his writings, in the famous book *"Historic Eight Documents"* which formed the basis of Naxalite Ideology. Naxalites organized the All India Co-ordination Committee of Communist Revolutionaries (AICCCR) and broke away from CPI (M). The organization was banned on July 4, 1975.

Initially the movement had centers at West Bengal, but in the recent years they have spread into less developed areas of rural central and eastern India i.e. Chatisgarh, Orissa, Andhra Pradesh, Jharkhanda, Madhya Pradesh etc., through the activities of underground groups like CPI (Marxist). The CPI (Marxist) and some other Naxal factions are considered as terrorists by the government of India and various State governments. Maoist Communist Centre, Dakshin Desh Group, People's War Group, Andhra Revolutionary Communist etc., are several disputing factions in this regard. In 1980's it was estimated that around 30 Naxalite groups were active with 30, 000 active members. In 2004, it was estimated by the Home Ministry of India that The Naxalites were equipped with 6500 regular weapons besides a large number of unlicensed country made arms. One fifth of the Naxal groups are active in forest and hill areas of 160 administrative districts India. In Orissa, Bansdhara Group, People's Liberation Guerrilla Army (PLGA) and CPI (M), Janasakti are active in their operation.

The activities of Naxal are negative, suppressive and destructive. Despite their ideology, they have over the years become just another terrorist outfits, extorting money from middle level land owners and worse over extorting and dominating lives of the Adivasis and villagers who they claim to represent in the name of providing justice. They affect the unarmed and innocent civilians and Armed Police, Special Operation Groups, and CRPF Jawans also. In July 2008, they even attacked the Greyhound Force at Malakanagiri. They attacked more than 70 policemen, 17 security personnel and many more suspected civilians and police informer in 2008. They wiped out life and loot the armed weapons and created untold miseries to different sections of society. They are far from their very ideological activities now. All Naxal groups at the inception had vehemently denounced the CPI (M) for participating in Parliament elections. Boycott of the Parliament was the sine-qua-non of Naxalism. However, the retreat from this aspect of petty bourgeois revolution has led to bitterness divisions among the Naxalites. Now-a-days they are engaged in kidnapping civil and police officials, keeping them as hostages and claiming the release of particular Naxals from jail. In the present situation, we are confronted with the menace of Naxalism in a big way and how to deal with it still remains in dilemma for us.

From past few years, women Naxal ideologues have been formed to further invigourate the Naxal insurgency in India. Usually the lady Naxals are involved in under-ground activities which are a part of their network. Women cadre Naxal groups mainly works for Nari Mukti Sangh. There are women leaders who work as area commander in different parts of the Naxal affected regions. Their main intention is to secure the basic rights for women.

The other issues handled by the women community include claiming compensation/rehabilitation package promised by the government and public relations exercise with police officials to reduce police harassment of surrendered Naxalites. To marry Adivasi girls forcibly by kidnapping them is a common practice among tribals. There is no barrier for a male person to marry the number of women. There is no alternative for a woman rather to reconcile the situation in fear of physical torture. Gradually the uprising began among Adivasi women due to such forcible marriage. They fought against such type of oppression and injustice. In due course of time the number of women cadre increased among Naxals especially in Dandakaranya known as *Krantikari Adivasi Mahila Sangh*. Among the entire Naxal groups 30 per cent constitute the women cadets.

Most of the women even teenaged girls are the victims of circumstances. One of the teenaged girls named Laxmi of Kareemnagar district of Andhra Pradesh confessed that, "Comrades visited over villages for food provisions, medical help and other needs. I joined the movement as a courier for the Maoists. I was an orphan."

Women like Sunita, Pramila, Jaya, in Andhra Pradesh and Pratima Das, Mala, Rakhi, Prachi, Jyoti in Orissa are such type of victims. Mala led women cadres in Orissa and Sobha worked as area commander and arrested in 2006. All learn running, jumping, crawling, jogging and firing the forest.

A maoist cadre woman named Sini Sai, the mother of Bhagaban Sai of Kalinganagar in the Jajpur district of Orissa demonstrated her boldness during an interview. She confessed that, "We will confront the police till our last breath."

Most of the women Naxalites are talented and dedicated. At times they are killed in exchange of fire with the police or arrested by the police. Women hold up half of the sway in PLGA. In India there are overall 40 per cent women Naxalite warriors and in some places even they crossed 50 per cent. Some times it was eye witnesses during their mass operation like Nayagarh attack. Gradually the Naxlites approached and attracted the women cadre as a symbol of inspiration. It is ascertained from different sources that there is no sexual disparity. All are living as comrades with equal status.

The increasing growth and widespread activities of Naxalites irrespective of man and women definitely may bring a new change in the society. To further the development of the present scenario we have to adhere to the real and rational norms of the present society. After all and above all, we have to fight unto the last for our well survival selflessness and loveness.

REFERENCES

Anupam Bharat, Oriya daily, 6/9/08.

Anwesha-7, Oriya Monthly, September, 2001.

Indian Express, Bhubaneswar, 18/7/2008/, 14/8/2008/28/8/2008. 11/9/2208.

Internet.

Khabar, Oriya daily, 26/8/2008, 14/9/2008.

Nisan, Oriya Quarterly, January-March, 2007.

11

NAXALS DEVASTATED SOCIAL PEACE

Rajib Lochan Panigrahy

The foremost importance task of the state is to give security for their citizens. Now-a-days external aggression and internal rebellion became a challenge to government. Social disturbance leading to unemployment, atrocities, for earning easy money has devastated the social peace. From time to time in the name and fame of Naxals, some anti-social people are taking profits in cash and kind from the public. In some areas few scrupulous people also exploiting social beings in the name of Naxal. The Naxal activities and their movements has becoming alarming to the Central and State Government, paramilitary, military, armed forces and related authorities, etc. The life span of people became short. The social life became precious in terrorist and Naxal attacks in most of the State in India. It became very much expensive to the Government.

Out of 30 States, 20 are naxal dominated States. Among of 604 districts, 259 districts are Naxal prone. In between 2001-06, India faced 3,37,000 attacks in which 3,200 number of para-military and armed persons, 9,100 civilians died. In counter-attacks 11,600 Naxals and terrorists have been demises. There are 7700 number of Naxal attacks happened in this period, 600 police and paramilitary person, 2000 civilian, 1000 Naxals has been died. In the country there are 5 Naxal and 12 terrorist organizations working who terrified civil society of India and made challenge to Government. For the maintenance of developmental works and cope with internal aggression became a hurdle to Government (Sambad, 29-8-2007).

The entire nation is afraid of Naxals. Naxals are alarming to Government as they will be endangered to civil society and Government machinery. It is increasing day by day and became alarming in recent years. As on survey, from 2004-2008, Naxal induced states of India faced the victims of Naxal attacks. It had occurred death of 912 civilians and 590 police and military persons engaged in Naxal operations or living in naxal dominated areas. On Government report 926 Naxals has been died in this period (Sambad, 29-5-2007).

The following table clearly depicts the deceased persons in Naxal victims:

Year	*2004*	*2005*	*2006*	*2007*	*2008**
Civilian	101	223	266	240	72
Security Personnel	89	113	128	218	42
Naxals	69	201	348	192	115

* up to May' 2008.

It seems that out of Naxal dominated States AP, Orissa, Jharkhand, Chhattisgarh is facing more Naxal attacks. Both States and Central governments are more alert on Naxal activists. Since, a decade, out of 13 Naxal dominated States, menace of Naxal violence and attacks prevailed in more limited States such as Bihar, Jharkhand, Orissa, Chhattisgarh, A.P., W.B, and eastern Maharasthra.

The State confronts a wide range of internal threats and security problems. For tackling the Naxal attacks and for maintenance of a peaceful social life, state and centre cooperation is quite essential. Naxalism became disaster which distresses the social mass. The Naxals are living in hilly, forest areas with the people living in that locality in any way. The local people are generally tribals, dalits, and minorities. They are encouraging these people by persuading the local rich people, politician, government servants who are violating their rules to facilitating them, exploiting them, cheating them without providing their legitimate rights, benefits and privileges etc. The involvement of these people gives existence in that locality and enriches the Naxal movements. The Naxal movements and attacks are only for agitation against lack of social developmental works and defects in it, problems and insufficiency in public distribution system, displacement, rehabilitation and resettlement, unemployment and under employment situations, atrocities and extractions from lower castes, *dalits* by higher caste, rich, political people, officers, defects in government machinery, exploitation and punishment by local police and other authorities, defects in law and order situations, etc. In Toto the Naxal movements started to face the monopolies of government officials, mal-functioning in implementation of government schemes and defective government policies.

Terrorism leads to dalits and minorities. The division rule framed by terrorists for social and government level devastations due to defective government policy and secularist State such as India. Human wants are unlimited and opportunities and facilities can not be fulfilled for men what they wants. Naxals convincing by anyway to dalits and Naxals that they are deprived of scarcities and neglected by government officials, village level politicians, bureaucrats, higher level politicians in ruling government, exploited by rich people, etc. They are training their members' everyday, making diagrams how to attack the government offices, police stations/centers, civil societies, disturb in roadways, railways, government systems, to fulfill targets, to lout/theft property from government godowns, rich families, construction houses, paramilitary houses, etc. In such situations, terror spreads among the civil society and many times it is seen civil innocent people dies. They are equipped with high volume and latest bombs, arms, ammunitions which government does not have. Their targets are practical having no failures. The do not fail in their mission Orissa faced such situations. The Nayagarh Naxal attack, Malkanagiri anti-blast vehicle explosion, Balimela Naxal boat bombing, Motu and Kalimela police attack, etc. has astonished the government machinery and spread terror in the society which are evidentiary for fulfilling their mission. Nayagarh is a place which is neither nearer to Naxal districts such as Rayagada, Koraput, Malkangiri, Nawarangapur, nor nearer to states like Andhra Pradesh, Madhya Pradesh, Chhattisgarh, Bihar, West Bengal. Nayagarh is not a tribal dominated district and is nearer to state capital Bhubaneswar. Naxal attack on police training centre at Nayagarh has created the platform for Naxal movement in Ganjam district in ghumusar are and they have created a new district viz. Ghumusar Naxal district. Because they can marched the Ghumusar area and Ganjam-Kandhamal boarder where encounters made between Naxals and police. They are picked up all the amunities from Nayagarh polic godown and kept advanced amunities, thrown all the traditional weapons and rifles at the jungle of Ganjam-Kandhamal boarder. After Naxal-police war, many Naxal and few police died. Cumbing operation became more acute by special police force find few vehicles theft was kept half-burnt, many police weapons and articles in that mountain. Since, than Naxal made their base at kandhamal district. It is astonished that they have proper knowledge about the advanced weapons in that training centre which they have succeed in their mission to lout. They have targeted Ganjam district which became a challenge to Ganjam Police. After that attack they have targeted different places, police stations to attack which made terror among the social people through their threatening posters in public places. Since, that period, Kandhamal riots among dalits and minorities grown up, firing-bombing became day-to-day affiar, many killed which becomes a national and international issue, many military-paramilitary staff died, many Naxals encountered. It became a threat to the neighboring districts. Even the vehicles passing through the district has been cancelled their route for around a month because passengers hesitate to travel through this route.

Naxal violances increases due to SEZ led displacement of tribals in different areas of Orissa like Kalinga Nagar. A mass struggle has occurred in Kalinga Nagar between tribals and officials in the charge of SEZ and company people. The south Orissa, West Orissa and Jajpur, Dhenkanal, Keonjhor district of North Orissa has been dominated by Naxal violence which threatened the paramilitary department of orissa and became challenge to the CRPF jawans, Rapid Action Force, Black Commando, military persons of Government of India. Leading to POSCO Project, Jagatsinghpur has also occurred Naxal violence. The four districts of North Orissa has disturbed by Naxals due to tribal displacements. So, Government of Orissa has declared the four districts as Naxal prone district.

The following violences, demises, loses occurred in year 2008:

1. January 12 - Ammunition factory identified, 5 Naxals arrested, 18 lakh rupees ceased.
2. January 20 - 4 districts of North Orissa declared as Naxal prone district.
3. January 28 - Explosive items identified under earth for explosion kept by Naxals.
4. February 01 - 3 forest guards killed in Dhenkanal by Naxals.
5. March 02 - Encounter by Malkangiri police, 3 Naxal died by police encounter.
6. March 03 - Police outpost fired by Naxals at Sambalpur.
7. April 24 - Landmine blast at Kalimela, one died.
8. April 29 - Police Sub-inspector, 2 Naxals died at MV97 of Malkangiri.

9. May 09 - Forester killed on firing by Naxals.
10. May 10 - Land mine blast at Mourbhanj.
11. June 06 - Kenduleaf godawn burnt down.
12. June 10 - 2 Moists/Naxals dead in encounter.
13. June 22 - Killing by cutting of throat by Moist.
14. June 27 - Burning of truck, firing in Sambalpur city by Naxals.
15. June 04 - Former Niab-Sarapanch killed by Naxal on firing.

North Orissa districts are dominated by MCC and South Orissa districts dominated by PWG activists. Leftists increased in Orissa who have their committees in Andhra Pradesh-Orissa boarder. South Orissa is the base of Naxals because of boarder of AP-Orissa which is hilly forest area in the districts of Rayagada, Malkangiri, Nawarangapur, Koraput. The Naxal devastations have done their attacks, bomb blasts, explosions more in Malkangiri, Nawarangapur, Rayagada, Koraput districts. The explosion in Malkangiri are growing up. So, Government has delivered an anti-blast military vehicle which was supplied for Naxal operation by military forces which was burst by land mine blast while the military people marching on road, which is totally lost by blast. In this situation Government of India Military Department has been astonished. They are trying to made more protected vehicle that the vehicle lost. It is evidentary that Naxals are more intelligent that military. It became a challenge to GoI and India Defence wing. AP police got information that Naxals have their training and safe residing place at the mountain in the Chitrakonda Dam. When they are marching in a boat, no Naxal found after several searching. When they returning back Naxals made blast by throwing bombs and the entire boat and the jawans has been missed. After searching by special forces on water and air, broken boat has been found from the ground of the dam in the water and few dead bodies found in complete and some others found in partial which are eaten by fish and some others are still under search. It became a challenge both for AP and Orissa Government. Every day in Kandhamal, Malkangiri, Rayagada, Koraput, Kalahandi there is an Naxal attack which covers the media and some are not under publicity.

REFERENCES

Behera, Manas, "Challenges of Naxalite Violence in Orissa", *South Asian Politics*, New Delhi, May'2008, p. 14-15.

Mukharjee, Uddipan — "Maoism and Its Future in India", South Asian Politics, New Delhi, July' 2008, p. 24-25.

Sambad (Oriya Daily), 01.01.2008.

Sambad (Oriya Daily), 29.08.2007.

Sambad (Oriya Daily), 29.05.2007.

Sambad (Oriya Daily), 03.09.2007.

Yojana (Oriya Edition-Spl. issue on Naxalism), Feb. 2007.

Yojana (English Edition-Spl. issue on Naxalism), Feb. 2007.

12

NAXALITE VIOLENCE IN ORISSA

Manas Behera

ABSTRACT

The Naxal attack in Nayagarh has once again brought back the issues of naxalism and of naxal violence into the Centre-state of politics in Orissa. The annual budget that the State government presented became a non-issue under the shadow of this event. The time is now ripe for a serious, objective analysis of the situation to develop a correct strategy towards resolving the problem. The State Government should take the initiative in the matter. It must have the boldness to admit its own mistakes and should have the courage to go beyond the stereo type paradigm of considering it as a law and order problem.

Hundreds of naxals successfully carried out their biggest ever attack in the state in Nayagarh town in the late night of 15th February, killing fifteen policemen and one civilian. They were able to take away a huge number of arms from the police armory and attacked the police training school, police stations of Nayagarh, Dasapallah, Nugaon and Mahipur out-post. The entire state was shocked as this is unprecedented in the history of the state in terms of its target, location, strategy and effect. Nayagarh is only about 85 kms away from the State capital, Bhubaneswar and does not come under the naxal affected districts of the State. Another new dimension of this attack in the State is the involvement of a large number of its cadre's. The complete failure of the intelligence to anticipate such a big attack and the much hyped biggest hi-tech anti-naxal operation's failure to capture any speaks of the State Government approach to the problem. The stereotype approach is not going to bring any tangible result in finding the root cause of this problem and in developing correct strategy to solve it. Any strategy in this regard must go beyond the law and order paradigm as this has failed not only in the state but in other parts of the country as well.

Naxalism and the related violence stems from a particular ideology of revolutionary violence born out of the Naxalbari uprising in West-Bengal in 1967. It believes in armed struggle to seize state power to transform the existing socio-political structure. However, there was a division in the naxal movement on the issue of violence and the CPI(ML) liberation accepted the parliamentary path. The PWG and the MCC and some other groups practiced violence. The people's war group and the MCC merged with each other creating the new one, CPI (maoist) in 16th September, 2004. Violence has become the identity of naxal politics in India and also in Orissa, thus redefining the concept of revolutionary violence. The Nayagarh incident only reiterates this understanding. Violence as the only method of Maoist politics is neither politics nor Maoist. It is a kind of violent anarchism. In the words of Lenin, 'Anarchism is a product of despair, failure to understand the class struggle of the proletariat, absurd negation of politics in bourgeois society . . . subordination of the working class to bourgeois politics in the guise of negation of politics.' The violence of the naxals does not espouse the cause of revolutionary politics in the state. It fails to help the people in organizing struggles on issues that affect their life and living. The naxals ignore or are unable to comprehend the political space that the present bourgeoisie system has for the common, marginalized people, though limited it is. This leads to the negation of the struggle of the masses of the deprived classes. The violence has degenerated into killing of petty officials; 'informers' etc.This is a parochial, distorted practice of revolutionary strategy.

The prime-minister has described the naxal violence as the, 'single biggest internal security challenge'. But the response of the Indian state to deal with this challenge is seriously flawed, so also the approach of the Orissa Government. The naxals have presence in more than 165 districts in the country and in more than half of the districts in Orissa. The naxal movement in Orissa started way back in 1968 and had no such widespread presence as it is today.The State Government banned the organization in 2006.The approach of the State Government towards the naxal problem is incapable of going beyond the 'law and order paradigm'. This paradigm has failed in containing, not to talk of resolving the problem, the growth of naxal violence in the state in the past 40 years. Rather it has helped in isolating the common, deprived masses from the political system, making them more accessible to the naxals and their ideology. The naxal problem is a multi-dimensional socio-economic problem with an interplay of many factors and forces. The common minimum programme of the UPA Government at the center has under lined this fact by stating in the programme that it is not merely a law order problem, but a deeper socio-economic issue. But neither the Central Government nor the State Government seem to have learnt anything from this reality. Secondly, the issue of democratic and participatory planning and development gets a secondary treatment in the present official discourse. The growth of the naxal movement and of violence has a direct link with the underdevelopment, marginalization, exclusion of the people, particularly of the poor tribal. The underdeveloped, backward districts are marked by naxal presence. These areas are rich in mineral and other natural resources. Despite investments by the governments in these areas, nothing substantial has been achieved in the development of the living conditions of the poor, exploited people. The developmental paradigm that the Government is pursuing does not challenge the existing power structure, nor empower the poor people. Rather it reinforces the dominance of the local elite who are also linked to the ruling classes in the State. They sustain each other and the developmental process serves them. A small elite is accommodated from the marginalized, who happens to be the by-product of the developmental process. The big dams, industries, mining projects in these areas have displaced the local people from their land and livelihood and makes them wage labors in these projects. Deforestation also leads to migration of these people into industries. The rehabilitation and resettlement of the displaced people in the State has been a painful experience since past fifty years due to lack of political will, bureaucratic and inhuman approach of the State. The history of re-settlement in Orissa is the history of betrayal by the State. The Hirakud dam, Rourkela Steel Plant, M.C.L.etc. are examples of this sad story. So any new promise of resettlement is seen with suspicion by the people to be displaced in the proposed new projects. Another problem is the undemocratic, authoritarian, oppressive attitude of the state towards the democratic movement of the people to be displaced. The police firing in Kalinganagar, Maikanch, etc. has helped in isolating these people further. The displaced people don't have a say in the decision making process of setting up of industry or in displacement. The official discourse of development suffers from lack of understanding of objective ground reality. It speaks in terms of budgetary allocations, growth rate, etc which ignores the real living conditions of the poor. The nexus of contractor-corrupt officer-politician takes away a big share of the money for development. The money-lenders exploit the poor tribal people in the absence of state intervention. Mostly the exploiters are non-tribal and non-local people for which the situation becomes more complex Corruption and bureaucratic attitude of the administration only helps in alienating the people from the system. The governance system doesn't exhibit sufficient space to accommodate the poor, mariginalised people, rather they are thrown away or are deprived of their dues. The current development discourse in the state is based on the neo-liberal recommendations of the World Bank, MF. It recommends for the retreat of the state from social sectors like health education, social security, etc. This has left the poor, mariginalised people more helpless in the face of the offensive of the market forces. The aggressive zeal that the State Government has shown in industrialization and in the exploitation of natural resources with the involvement of big capitalists, has little scope for the state's concern for the affected people in this process. All these create; sustain sufficient ground for the growth of naxal activities. Naxalism is based on a particular ideology. The objective socio-economic conditions in the state provides the ground for this ideology. Unless this is understood, there is no way to overcome it. So far, the govt. has failed to evolve a comprehensive strategy, except taking it from a security perspective. The Government seems to be a victim of the 'grey-hound' model of dealing with the naxalite violence. Spending money on development of the backward areas will not help alone, unless supplemented by the strategy of empowerment through a participatory, transparent, democratic, accommodative system of governance. The power structure should be dismantled in favor of the marginalized. The initiative should come from the Government, but there seems to be no such possibility at present. The other democratic parties, groups and forces should build a broad based movement on this issue to force the Government to change its present policy. The left should take the lead which has failed so far. The naxals should learn from the Nepal experiment and rethink on the strategy of violence. They should mobilize their strength on building a broad, powerful, democratic people's movement with other forces for a people's alternative. Militancy is necessary and welcome in building a people's movement on people;s issues,but unnecessary and mindless violence only helps the authoritarian forces and harms the cause of the movement. The state govt. seems determined not to learn anything from Nayagarh as seen from the post-Nayagarh responses of the State Government.

13

NAXALISM
BIGGEST THREAT TO INDIA'S INTERNAL SECURITY

Dr. Saroja B

The country is dealing with not one but two wars within its own borders. The first as we all know is the rising threat of Islamic terrorism, but the second often overlooked dimension to this internal war, is that of the Naxalite terrorists, who are bred and sustained by the Communists of India, CPI (ML). The present day scenario is even more sinister as both of these anti national groups have begun conspiring in an elaborate pattern of mayhem and terror which now threatens to overpower India at the grass root level.

The Naxalite movement, starting from a small village on the tri-junction of India, Nepal and what was then East Pakistan in 1967, spread like wildfire to different parts of the country. The movement is today a complex web that covers some 194 districts in 18 States of India.

A cycle of violence and bloodshed is being unveiled across the rural landscape of middle-India. The result has been that rural India is as unruly as it has never been.

MAJOR PROBLEMS

Land is the vital issue for Maoist since the movement launched in Naxalbari village was for land. Land reforms and its judicious distribution have not been implemented in many of the affected states, particularly Andhra, Orissa and Chhattisgarh. Another problem in tackling this menace is that these naxal groups are not coming to the table for talks and their ideology is steeped in armed revolution. They want to transmute the social structure through the barrel of the gun. Further they are getting moral and material support from far flung centers. They have links with LTTE, a terrorist organisation operating in Sri Lanka. Right since the inception of this movement China is furnishing tacit support to it.

Added to this they operate forest areas and in many cases from inaccessible terrain.

MAIN FEATURES

The disturbing features of the movement are:

Spread over a large geographical area;

Increase in potential for violence;

Unification of PW and MCCI;

Plan to have a Red Corridor;

Nexus with other extremist groups.

Violence has peaked in India from Maoist or Naxalite violence being more dangerous to India's national security than either Pakistan, or insurgents in Kashmir and north-east states.

Violence has ever since taken a high trajectory, as the following figures show:

Total	*Incidents*	*Deaths*
2001	1,208	564
2002	1,465	482
2003	1,597	515
2004	1,533	566
2005	1,608	677
2006	1,509	678
2007	1,565	696

There are dozens of complaints pending with the National Human Rights Commission and State Human Rights Commissions against alleged fake encounters. In response, Naxals are toughening their stand and adding to the violence in an already volatile situation. Intelligence agencies have for long also been warning that Indian Naxal groups are working with the Communist Party of *Nepal* (Maoists) to create a "Compact Revolutionary Zone" (CRZ) that spreads from Nepal into Bihar and Andhra Pradesh. "That is a theoretical proposition but it definitely gives an idea of how wide-spread the Naxals are in the subcontinent," says a senior intelligence officer. The "Combat Revolutionary Zone" (CEZ) spreads from Nepal through Bihar and the Dandakaranya region of Andhra Pradesh. The Naxals are now engaged in plugging gaps in north Bihar and North Chhattisgarh to complete the CRZ, says the officer. The Naxal movement is also powerful in Orissa, Chhattisgarh, Madhya Pradesh, Uttar Pradesh and other parts of central India. These are also areas where India's most precious assets are located. "All these areas (are) where greater part of India's mineral resources, hydro-electric and other resources are located," Prime Minister Manmohan Singh admitted. Ultimately the Indian democracy will prevail, believe analysts within the government and outside.

Even the large number of casualties caused during elections received scant attention thus highlighting lack of public support to the anti-Naxal forces police and para military. There is a need to completely change this approach. Greater public concern would provide for the police and the paramilitary fighting the Naxals required wherewithal for combating the ills of militancy. While this has received financial approval its implementation has been tardy leading to large money allotted for modernization unspent.

The best government talent in the country is in the civil services including the police, the Indian Police Service. Yet the fate of the counter Naxal forces remains that of peripheral fighters. It is time they are given the centre stage for the war against Naxalism is as much our fight as theirs.

The Government of India have already expressed concern over the spread of the Naxalite movement over a huge geographical area. The Prime Minister described Naxalite movement as the single biggest threat to the internal security of the country.

The Naxals' potential for violence has increased substantially with their acquisition of sophisticated weapons and expertise in the use of improvised explosive devices (IEDs). They are said to be in possession of at least 6,500 regular weapons including AK 47 rifles and SLRs. They have built this arsenal essentially by looting weapons from police/ landlords, purchasing them from smugglers, acquiring from insurgent groups like the NSCN (IM) and ULFA and also obtaining some weapons from Nepal.

The movement got a tremendous boost when its two major components, the People's War (PW) and the Maoist Communist Centre of India (MCCI), decided to merge on March 21, 2004, though a formal announcement was made on October 14, 2004 only. The unified party was called the Communist Party of India (Maoist). The merger, apart from augmenting the support base of the movement, has given it the character of a pan-Indian revolutionary group. The Naxals' plan to have a Compact Revolutionary Zone stretching from Indo-Nepal border to the Dandakaranya Region is likely to get a fillip with the unification of their ranks.

The Naxalite groups' nexus with the other extremist organizations has added to the complexity of the problem. There are indications that the PWG cadres received training in the handling of weapons and IEDs from some ex-LTTE cadres. They have also some understanding with the National Socialist Council of Nagaland (I-M) to support each others' cause. Some batches of CPML-Party Unity also appear to have received arms training under the guidance of United Liberation Front of Assam. The Communist Party of India (Maoist) has close fraternal relations with the Communist Party of Nepal (Maoist) also.

The government plans to combat the Naxal problem appear generally sound on paper. However, there is a huge gap between the formulation of policies and their implementation at the ground level. According to the latest findings of the National Sample Survey Organization (NSSO), the number of people living below the poverty line (BPL) stood at 22.15% in 2004-05, a slight improvement over 26.09% in 1999-2000. The situation is compounded by the mismatch between growth and its distribution resulting in accentuation of economic disparities. Economists agree that uneven growth often leads to social unrest. There are remote areas where there is hardly any governance.

It would thus appear that the factors which gave rise to Naxalism – the extent of poverty, uneven development, poor governance, neglect of land reforms, rising unemployment and tribals getting a raw deal - are, unfortunately, very much present today also. Unless these basic issues are sincerely addressed, a security-centric approach by itself would not be enough to deal with the problem.

Index